Farrakhan, Islam &
The Religion
That Is Raping
America

Moody Adams

Cover drawing by Brandi Downs

Contents

Foreword

This book was conceived on October 16, 1995, the day of the Million Man March. The statement of purpose for the march was noble and fine. The behavior of the vast crowd was admirable. But when they began the ceremony the audience, which included hundreds of thousands of Christians, bowing their heads and repeated a prayer to Allah from the *Quran.* I thought of Israel turning "quickly" away from their god to worship a false idol god at the base of Sinai's mountain. My heart went out to God. I thought how distressed and angry He was over Israel's idol worship and how upset he must be over America's new found idol worship.

As Washington's mayor told the crowd in the mall we all worship the same God, just by different names, it dawned upon me how successfully Islam has deceived American Christians. Our country is not aware of the vast and deadly difference between the teachings of Islam and Christianity.

Jesus Christ repeatedly and viciously attacked false religion. America's religious leaders have failed to follow His example, choosing to be more conciliatory. This has made it possible for Islam to become America's fastest growing religion and engulf millions of souls here in the United States.

After the march, Farrakhan emerged as the pre-eminent leader of America's black people. It became apparent that all the efforts of Martin Luther King, Jr.'s success in moving towards intergration and improving the condition of his people are in danger of being overthrown by this separatist. Farrakhan, who has taken the same stand as the KKK, wants complete separation of the two races.

When Farrakhan followed up his march with a meeting with Gadhafi, Sadaam Hussein and other leaders of terrorist, Muslim nations, it raised the Islamic threat to a new level. Gadhafi, a sponsor of world-wide terrorism, pledged one billion dollars to help Farrakhan destabilize the government of the United States. It left no room for doubt about the intentions, nor potential of Louis Farrakhan. He wants the present government of the United States destroyed. Joined with the same crowd that is terrorising Israel, Farrakhan is a force for us to be concerned about.

John Conybeare, a seventeenth century English theologian wrote, "We oughtt not to be careless and indifferent about the future. But as there are goods in life possible to be obtained, and evils capable of being avoided, so we should provide ourselves with proper means to obtain the one and escape the other.... If we neglect our own interest, we deserve the calamities which come upon us."

Hopefully, this book will provide a solution that will help us escape a future calamity, such as racial dissension, spiritual deception and national disorder could bring.

Shipping Instructions for LADYJANE

Print this Packing Slip and enclose inside the front cover of the book.

Please ship this item no later than Thu Jul 16, 2026.

Ship to:

ALIBRIS APEX DC 76524205-35
APEX
800 AVONDALE AVE.
GRANDVIEW HEIGHTS, OH 43212-3473
UNITED STATES

PN #	Item ID	Alibris ID	Media Type	Title / Author	Seller List Price	Order Date
76524205-35	6544	B083661140	BOOK	Farrakhan, Islam & the Religion That is Raping America Adams, Moody	$6.95	Jul, 6 2026

Chapter 1
Gadhafi's Revenge

"God will destroy America by the hands of Muslims," promised Louis Farrakhan. " God will not give Japan or Europe the honor of bringing down the United States; this is an honor God will bestow upon Muslims." With these words, spoken while visiting Libya, Farrakhan joined with Sadaam Hussein and Gadhafi in seeking to undermine the government of the United States.

"If we Muslims can come together all over the world, we could become the superpower of the 21st century. And that is the fear in the West," Louis Farrakhan declared to a gathering of students from Ghana, Nigeria and Uganda meeting in Malaysia. "Those who fear Islam fear that Islam is going to replace the Western hegemony in the world, and they are right."

These statements clarified the objective of Farrakhan and Islam during his 20-nation tour in January and February of 1996 and forced Americans to look at America's Muslim leader in an entirely different light.

Farrakhan looks more and more like a degenerate raping America's Lady Liberty; disrespectfully forcing himself upon her and ripping away her virtue. His supporters look more like the gang that held the lady down. Gadhafi, it appears, is just paying the motel bill while his friend Farrakhan violates Miss. Liberty.

Columnist Ken Hamblin wrote, "I wonder whether the

liberals and so-called disenfranchised African Americans who allowed themselves to be caught up in the sorrowful 'atonement' of black men last October 16 have yet come to grips with the possibility they may have been duped by Louis Farrakhan and his infamous Million Man March. If they haven't questioned Farrakhan's supposed good intentions by now, maybe his latest deal with the devil will be food for thought."

Farrakhan's deal with the devil
opens a new Muslim front against the U.S.

Farrakhan said his "world friendship tour" to Iran, Libya, Sudan, Nigeria, Syria, and other nations was intended to spread the message of self-help and personal responsibility that was voiced in October at the Million Man March in Washington. But critics suggest that Farrakhan's purpose was to raise money at a time when some commercial ventures linked to the Nation of Islam are in financial trouble.

Farrakhan did get the promise of large sums of money but he had to make a real deal with a bunch of real devils.

Libya

Following the Million Man March, Farrakhan received congratulations on its success from Libyan leader, Muammar Gadhafi. Libya is under a UN ban on arms sales and airline flights to Libya, which was imposed on April 15, 1992, because Gadhafi refused to turn over two Libyan security agents suspected of involvement in the 1988 downing of Pan Am flight 103 over Scotland.

Gadhafi invited Farrakhan to visit him in Libya. Farrakhan accepted and the meeting took place the week of January 22, 1996. At this meeting Gadhafi vowed to spend a billion dollars funding a Muslim lobby in the United States; he said he agreed with Louis Farrakhan efforts to fight the United States from the inside. The official Libyan news agency *JANA* made it clear that Gadhafi sees Farrakhan as a way to get into the American political process. "Our confrontation with America used to be like confronting a fortress from outside," Mr. Gadhafi told JANA. "Today we have found a loophole to enter the fortress and to confront it from within."

Gadhafi said the two men agreed to mobilize oppressed U.S. minorities in a "legal and legitimate form," establishing a black voting bloc that will be "stronger than the Jewish card in the election campaign."

It was in Libya that Mr. Farrakhan may have made the transition from social critic to foreign agent. He was reported to have been promised one billion dollars to "mobilize the oppressed minorities . . . to play a significant role in American political life. This is not Gadhafi's first generous gesture to Farrakhan. In 1984 he lent Mr. Farrakhan $5 million.

Reuters quoted Gadhafi as saying in Tunis, "American blacks could set up their own state within the United States with the largest black army in the world; because they have half a million blacks in the U.S. army."

The agency went on to say, "Farrakhan's meeting with Gadhafi 'incarnates' the leader of the oil-rich country's call last year to mobilize 10 million Muslims and Arabs in the United States."

Farrakhan was quoted as saying, "I am happy with the results of this meeting to unify Arabs, Muslims and Blacks and persecuted groups in America to play a strong role not only in the American elections but also in U. S. foreign policy."[1]

He said that when he made his appeal to Saddam for Muslims to unite, the Iraqi president responded, "Don't worry about the Arabs. We have fights, but in the end we will be united."

The Million Man March of Louis Farrakhan gave new hope to Muslim nations that their Islamic revolution was impacting America. It also brought hope to Gadhafi that he was about to get his revenge on the United States for their bombing attack on his country, thanks to Farrakhan.

Iran

Louis Farrakhan timed his visit to arrive in Tehran, Iran on February 10, 1996, the 17th anniversary of Ayatollah Khomeini's Islamic revolution. Farrakhan, accompanied by his 35-person delegation, joined in the celebration of the overthrow of Shah Mohammad Reza Pahlavi's pro-Western government. During that 1979 revolution, 52 U.S. hostages were held for over a year.

A Kuwaiti newspaper reports Mr. Farrakhan was the first foreigner to speak at the annual celebration, where tens of thousands chanted "Death to America."

As he celebrated the revolution, Farrakhan denounced the United States as "the Great Satan" and praised Iran's clergy-led government as a "perfect example of a government based on the Quran." While in Iran, Farrakhan attacked the U.S. Congress' decision to allocate $20 million for covert operations in Iran and promised any effort to destabilize the Islamic republic would not succeed. "Instead of allocating a budget to plot conspiracies against the Islamic system in Iran, the United States would do better to use the money to help homeless people in that country," Farrakhan told the Iranians.

Iran's President Hasherni Kafs praised Farrakhan and

said the Million Man March was proof that Iran's revolutionary message has been carried to all parts of the world. "An important point of the march, and one which must have been very bitter for the American (government) to swallow, were the Islamic manifestations of this congregation," said the President.

President Kafs expressed the delight of the Islamic world with the march, the rise of Farrakhan, and the possibility of a racial revolution that could bring down the government of the United States. He said "the U.S. government surely doesn't want to admit that this is related to the growing Islamic movement in the world ... carried from Iran to other countries ... our message is carried on the wings of angels. It is not confined to our geographical boundaries ... If anyone is alone, it is the arrogant American government."

Iraq

Farrakhan met with one of America's most bitter enemies, President Saddam Hussein, and denounced the U.S. policy he said is causing "mass murder" in Iraq. He pledged to work "nights and days marshaling the moral force that I believe is in all the American people to bring every pressure . . . on our government . . . that the mass murder of the Iraqi people must cease."

During his visit to Iraq, Farrakhan compared the deprivations of Iraqis living under U.N. economic sanctions with the fate of Jews in Nazi death camps. He denounced the United States as the "Great Satan" who had committed a "crime against humanity" by imposing sanctions on Iraq after the invasion of Kuwait in 1990.[2]

Farrakhan predicted his preachings would land him in prison when he got back home, saying that perhaps he would be jailed next to Sheik Omar Adbel-Rahman, the Egyptian cleric convicted in a plot to bomb landmarks in New York. "Maybe there's a cell next to Abdel-Rahman for me," Farrakhan said in a radio interview, "and maybe he and I will be together reading the *Quran* and encouraging each other."

His actions in Iraq stirred an outcry in the U.S. "Thousands of African American soldiers served their country in the Persian Gulf war in an effort to turn back the tyranny of Sadaam Hussein's ill conceived invitation," wrote Cristy Hardin Smith in *USA Today*. "Farrakhan's tour through the gutters of African and Middle Eastern political leadership has dishonored the achievements of these soldiers. African-American soldiers should speak out against a man who dares to call himself a leader, yet so easily breaks the laws of the nation they defend ... Farrakhan goes beyond free speech when he threatens national security by taking money from terrorist-supporting leaders," she wrote.[3]

Sudan

On February 8, Farrakhan stopped in Sudan and declared that Muslim fundamentalist leaders would prevail over the West. His visit came a day after Ambassador Timothy Carney was forced to leave the U.S. Embassy in Khartoum. The United States pulled out the embassy staff citing concerns for their safety. The State Department declared Sudan's government a sponsor of terrorism.[4]

The *Washington Times* commented, "yes, slavery is alive and well in North Africa, in Mauritania and the Sudan especially, and while the Nation of Islam leader is cavorting ... with the masters, abolitionists in the United States have had more than a bit of trouble trying to get anyone to listen to their tales of human bondage and slave trading." The *Times* said,

"Perhaps the real problem is that slavery in North Africa is not racial but religious. The master-slave relationship is not white-on-black but Black Muslims enslaving black Christians."[5]

Nigeria

In Nigeria, Farrakhan voiced support for the military government, which has refused to abide by the results of an election last June that was intended to restore democratic rule. The military ruler, Gen. Sani Abacha, seized power in a 1993 coup. He jailed opposition leaders and critical journalists and on November 10, 1995 he hanged Ken Sao-Wiwa and eight others who criticized his rule. Ken, a writer and environmental advocate, was demanding a greater share of oil revenues for his people.

"They said that you hanged one man," Farrakhan was quoted as saying, referring to countries that condemned the execution, "So what? Ask them, too, 'How many did you hang?' He said the government of Gen. Sani Abacha should be given a chance to return the West African country to democratic rule. Farrakhan said Moses was a dictator, and there were times when "stern discipline was needed." "Only in that military kind of way can a nation that has been down come up and get going," Mr. Farrakhan said.

Nigerian pro-democracy activists, who accused Farrakhan of wining and dining with their dictator, said, "We urge Farrakhan to ponder whether his famous march ... would have been possible if Americans were to be laboring under the yoke of military dictatorship."[6]

Last year, the Nigerian ambassador tried to donate $10,000 to the NAACP. The group returned the money, even though it is more than $3 million in debt. This black group wanted nothing to do with Farrakhan's new friend.

Reaction from the NAACP
the U.S. Government and others

Farrakhan's tour follows a tradition which goes back to a previous time when U.S. Black Muslims like boxer Muhammad Ali and Malcolm X received warm receptions in pro-Soviet Arab countries during the cold war with Russia. An angry reaction in the U.S. is also part of that tradition. Muslim leaders putting politics about their Islamic beliefs by honoring men who do not believe the basic truths of Islam, is also part of that tradition..

Kweisi Mfume, the new president and chief executive of the National Association for the Advancement of Colored People, said that Farrakhan's visits to countries that flout international standards did "not help" efforts to establish "conformity with international law."

Ronald Walters, chairman of the department of political science at Howard University, said regarding Farrakhan: "After the Million Man March, many thought they could welcome him into the pantheon of black leadership. Now they're finding out that consorting with him is not going to be as easy as they thought."

"Four months after his Million Man March edged him toward the political mainstream, Louis Farrakhan has touched off wide criticism with an extended world tour, which included countries the United States considers pariahs, and his bitterly anti-American remarks along the way," said Steven A. Holmes of the *New York Times*.

Rep. Peter King of New York has called for Mr. Farrakhan to be prosecuted for breaking U.S. laws. He said Farrakhan should be subpoenaed to testify before the House

International Relations human rights subcommittee. "There is no way that I will allow Farrakhan to skirt the law and continue to seek the financial backing of terrorist regimes to advance his racist political agenda," King said.

Mr. King is concerned that Farrakhan may have broken five laws: a requirement to register as a foreign agent; sanctions against Libya; restrictions on campaign contributions from foreign nationals; passport travel restrictions; and the Logan Act, which restricts private individuals from conducting foreign policy. "I've called on Janet Reno to launch a full investigation," Mr. King said "I've called on Janet Reno to investigate not just Farrakhan himself, but his entire evil empire."

The Jewish War Veterans voiced support for King's congressional investigations: "Farrakhan's cynicism would be comical if he weren't so dangerous," said Commander Goldman. "He claims the right to free speech as an American citizen, then vows the destruction of the United States at the hand of Muslims."

"It is shameful that an American citizen, much less a major religious leader in the United States, would cavort with dictators like Gadhafi and the Iranian leadership," State Department spokesman Nicholas Burns said. "The blood of Americans is on Gadhafi's hands, and it's on Iranian hands." The Justice Department's criminal division, which is investigating Farrakhan, informed him he may have to register as a foreign agent.

Randall Robinson, president of TransAfrica Forum, which lobbies on issues related to Africa and the Caribbean, was particularly upset at Farrakhan's support of Nigeria's military junta. "I am extremely disappointed with the statements made on this trip in countries like Nigeria and

Sudan," said Robinson. "His statements and the things that were said appear to make Minister Farrakhan an apologist for an authoritarian, corrupt, and repressive regime."

The White House denounced Farrakhan's trip. Presidential spokesman Mike McCurry said, "He met with some of the most brutal dictators and leaders of nations that the United States considers pariah states."

A defiant Farrakhan responded to his critics from Ankara, Turkey, saying, "I can go where I please and speak to anyone I please. I only have to answer to God." Upon his return to Chicago Farrakhan said, "You ruin the world and you're angry. I know why you're angry, because you see it slipping from your grip. These damnable liars have cast first. Bring me before Congress," he declared."[7]

Neil Goldman, National Commander of the Jewish War Veterans of the U.S.A., expressed amazement at Farrakhans tour, "A man will be judged by the company he keeps. Americans of all races, religions and ethnic backgrounds should regard as dangerous, a man whose friends and financial backers include the tyrants and terrorists in Libya, Nigeria, Iran, Iraq, Sudan, and the organizers of the World Trade Center bombing."[8]

Journalist Cal Thomas wrote, "Some of Louis Farrakhan's defenders had to swallow hard in the face of his condemnation of Jews, whites and the American system of government ... Now that Farrakhan has gone the extra mile and visited with the Libyan dictator and innkeeper to terrorists and murderers, Moammar Gadhafi, maybe they'll choke."[9]

Chapter 2
Middle East terrorist training in the United States

While Farrakhan plots the overthrow of the U.S. government by means of his new found political power, Islam is also operating on an older, quite different way – the terrorist front. While Farrakhan stirs up the black Americans against the United States, Middle East Muslims are stirring up Muslims to carry out terrorist activity against the United States.

Steven Emerson, who has reported on international terrorism for 10 years, said, "Jihad is a Holy war aimed at establishing the Islamic empire." On an astonishing PBS documentary on Islamic terrorism, he explained, "For these militants, jihad is a holy war to annihilate all non-believers (or infidels) and their ultimate goal is to establish an Islamic empire." The documentary traces the beginning of this world-wide effort in Afghanistan. When the Russians tried to take over this country, Muslims, with the help of three billion dollars funneled through Pakistan by the CIA, defeated the Russians and forced their withdrawal. Charles Cogan, a former CIA official, said this was the most successful overt action during the cold war. The victory drew a shout which echoed throughout the Muslim world that not even a "super-power" could defeat the armies of Allah. They were convinced nothing could stop them again.

But these Muslims which were headquartered in Pakistan, did not fight the Russians only. After their victory against Russia, they turned their guns in the name of jihad, they moved against Christians, Jews and moderate Muslims. The CIA was putting up the front money for this organization with the idea of stopping Russian expansion. But the Muslim revolutionaries, using their natural cunning, funneled a large part of the money toward the world-wide revolution of Islam.

President Mubarak of Egypt calls the so-called Afghani veterans the main terrorist threat to the stability of his government. One of the two assailants killed in October, 1993 in an attempt on the life of the Interior Minister Hassan al-Alfi was a veteran of the Afghan war.

In Algeria several hundred Muslim-Arab veterans are fighting in the ranks of the Islamic Salvation Front. In Tunisia these veterans are also supporting An-Nahda, a Muslim extremist faction in that country.

Ayatollah Khomeni's take-over of Iran inflamed the anti-western passions of Muslims to do the same throughout the world. The fire continued to rise in 1981 when the assassination of President Anwar Sadat of Egypt by Muslim militants convinced the Muslim militants that no world leader could defy them.

The Secret Invasion

With their new-found confidence, they invaded the U.S. masked as "Freedom Fighters" working to help the Palestinian cause. They found the United States was the best and easiest country in the world to raise money, enlist soldiers, produce training videos, teach their terrorists how to use firearms and how to make and use bombs. In the United States, the land of freedom and opportunity, they obtained favorable publicity to build their platform for world revolution.

The PBS documentary reported, "Thirty Islamic terrorist groups are working in America with non-profit status; under the guise of raising money for hospitals and child care, however, most of the funds go to buy weapons."

According to law enforcement officials Muslims are training for warfare in at least nine sites in the United States; and are discharging 1,000 rounds of ammunition every weekend. The FBI says these terrorists have well-disguised command and communication centers. In Texas they operate out of a hamburger stand. In Chicago their front is a grocery store.

Oliver Buck Revell, one of the FBI's top counter-terrorism agents, said, "What is unique is the international nature (of the Islamic terrorists)... Much more global than any terrorist network we have had to deal with in the past."

Abdullah Azzam, an extremist Muslim working out of the Mosque in Brooklyn, N.Y., said, "The fighting is obligatory on you wherever you can perform it. And just as when you are in America, you must fast ... so too must you wage jihad .... fighting with the sword." In 1989 Azzam was assassinated in Pakistan, making him a martyr to the Islamic cause.

Fayiz Azzam, the cousin of Azzam, told his 1990 audience in Atlanta, "Allah's religion, be praised, must offer scouts, must offer martyrs, blood must flow, there must be widows, there must be orphans, hands and limbs must be cut, and the limbs and the blood must be spread everywhere, in order that Allah's religion stand on its feet."

Tamim Al-Adnani, a prominent fund-raiser and recruiter for Islam in America, ordered his followers to train to kill, "Brothers, I encourage you to attend the firing practice. There is nothing greater than the power of the shot. Learn to shoot. The skill of shooting is so important ... From here we move on to the true shooting against the enemies of Allah."

El Sayyid A Nosair was arrested November, 1990 for the assassination of New York Rabbi Meir Kahane. The judge that tried him exclaimed that he had never before seen such hatred in a man. Nosair beat the manslaughter charges and was convicted only on possession of an illegal weapon.

The conspiracy
that was uncovered too late

In their investigation, the police found a huge amount of papers showing terrorists' plans, but they paid no attention to them at that time. Joseph Borrelli, of the New York police department, said, "There was no indication at all of any conspiracy of a nature that was spoken of. The facts indicate at this time that it was a lone gunman that committed the homicide."

Following Nosair's imprisonment, police officials ignored 47 boxes of personal possessions and papers in his home. Time would prove the law enforcement officials made a deadly mistake in disregarding this evidence which was obviously the records of extremists.

It was not until after the New York World Trade Center bombing that they read the 47 boxes of papers and discovered plans to blow up the Holland Tunnel, the Lincoln Tunnel, the United Nations building and assassination plans aimed at prominent United States citizens. They had overlooked one of the largest caches of terrorist materials ever found in the United States.

The most incriminating item among the papers was a

note which spelled out a plan for destroying the enemies of Allah. "We have to thoroughly demoralize the enemies of God ... by means of destroying and blowing up the towers that constitute the pillars...of their civilization such as the tourist attractions they are so proud of and the high buildings they are so proud of."

Michael Oherkasky, who was an investigator with the Manhattan District Attorney's office, said, "only when we started looking at that material and ...seeing things clearly for the first time did we become agitated because we had not seen it before, and excited because we now thought we had more of a clue about tracing the history of this group and more of an idea of what had actually happened here; in fact, it was a long term conspiracy that had been hatched by ... Rahman."

Allah's blind terrorist

Sheikh Omar Abdul Rahman, the blind teacher and Islamic extremist cleric, had come to the United States to become the leader of the Islamic terrorist movement. He said, "The obligation of Allah is upon us to wage jihad for the sake of Allah. It is one of the obligations which we must undoubtedly fulfill. And we conquer the land of the infidels and spread Islam by calling the infidels to Allah. And if they stand in our way, we wage jihad, for the sake of Allah."

In the summer of 1993, Rahman and nine followers were indicted for the bombing of the World Trade Center. They were also accused of planning to bomb the tunnels, the United Nations building and carry out assassinations. This group was broken up, but many others are carrying on the work of Islamic jihad across America. It is known that Sheik Rahman still provides leadership for terrorists from behind his prison walls.

**The worst Middle East terrorist
are training Americans in the United States**

Oliver Buck Revell, said, "The Hezbella and Hamas are very active in the United States. We now know that they have carried out military training operations, including firearm practice, the creation and construction of explosive devices and bombs. We know that they are taking munitions and materials into areas of the world where they are carrying out assassinations and acts of terrorism. They are also putting together arsenals within the United States for the same purposes."

In the Gaza strip, in December 1995, the leaders of Hamas asserted that the group will continue its jihad until all Palestine is liberated. One of their leaders, Mohammed Taha, gave a speech punctuated by taped gun fire and drove the crowd of 10,000 into a frenzy. A banner hanging over them proclaimed: "The killing of Jews brings people closer to God." Hamas opposes the Israeli-PLO autonomy agreement, and has killed scores of Israelis.

Officials acknowledge Hezballa and Hamas, the most radical of all Islamic terrorist groups, are very active in the United States. "We now know that they have carried out military training operations including fire arm practice, creation and construction of explosive devices and bombs... they are putting together arsenals in the Unites States."

IAP, with headquarters in Richardson, Texas, is Hamas' principal support group. Its literature urges, "Muslims to die in the Holy War against the Jews, the enemies of humanity, the bloodsuckers and the killers of prophets."

Sami Dhafar, the leader of Islamic Charity Project Intl., speaking in New York, 1992, said, "We want this small

Muslim community to serve as a dagger in the center of this civilization."

20/20 uncoveres how
Islam recruits in the United States

Muslims have opened another front against the U.S. – the recruitment front. They first convert Americans to Islam and then they turn them into enemies of the U.S. government. An interview with Tom Jarriel on ABC News 20/20, January 20, 1996, was an extraordinary and frightening account of a black man born and raised in the United States. They had to conduct a clandestine meeting in Jordan with David Belfield. David who later changed his name to Daoud Salahuddin slipped out of hiding in Iraq to tell this story without remorse or shame. He was recruited by Islamics connected with the regime of the Ayatollah Khomeni in Iran, together with many more young black American men.

Belfield, like so many young people at that time, was embittered by racism and the Vietnam war; and it was easy to recruit them for a cause they were told they could make a difference in. He converted to Islam and was trained as an assassin in the United States, then taken to Iran. He said he was chosen by the Revolutionary Council to kill a former Iranian ambassador, Ali Tabatabayi, who was an outspoken opponent of Khomeni and lived in the United States. Belfied carried out the assassination, killing Tabatabayi in cold blood outside his own front door.

He paid a postal worker to use his delivery truck and approached Tabatabayi's residence desguised as a post office worker carrying packages. Underneath the package was a gun. When Tabatabayi came to the door to sign for his package, Belfield looked him right in the eyes and pulled the trigger. He said from the look in his eyes it was evident he knew he was a man about to die. Tabatabayi fell to the floor of his home dead. Belfield escaped to Iraq, his assignment completed.

Belfield has eluded capture for fifteen years. He has collaborated in other assassintions and terrorist attacks world-wide with other black American men who were recruited by Iran and other Islamic countries. What seemed to appeal to these men was, as Belfield said in the interview, "We were involved in something big, that gives you a chance to earn some respect for yourself. We were exploited to a certain degree, yes."

Belfield is by no means the only such assassin. His friend, Clevin Holt who was once arrested for casing the presidential jet, Air Force One, has been tracked by authorities to Bosnia. Holt, operating under his Islamic name, Isa Abdullah fought against the Israelis in Lebanon, and was often seen outside the Marine compound in Beirut just before it was bombed in 1983.

In addition to the more subtle recruiting, you have men like Tamim Al-Adnani, a fund raiser and an open recruiter for the Islamic terrorists. He openly goes around the country appealing to angry Americans. Speaking to a Kansas audience in 1988, Al-Adnani said, "The only politics we understand is dat-dat-dat (automatic gunfire) ... we solve our problems in the trenches .... We will not stop, we will go up to the Muslim country of Russia, we will go down to Palestine ... any ruler who will not let us go, we will go by force – jihad."

The threat that is no laughing matter

Those who think the Islamic threat to the United States is laughable need to consider these facts. Their revolution succeeded in taking over the educated, advanced country of Iran. They have put the Sudan under Islamic law. They are exerting a strong influence in 42 countries where they are the majority religion.

Our mother country, England, is falling under Islam's influence. In 1985 an Islamic leader said, "If we can take London for Islam, we can take the world."[10] Today, Muslims outnumber evangelical Christians in England. Arab Muslims own a large percentage of the valuable real estate in London.

Ten years ago, London's great Harrods department store was purchased by Mohammed al-Fayed, who also owns the fabled Ritz Hotel in Paris and one-time front man for the Sultan of Brunei. Fayed socializes with the Prime Minister and other prominent politicians as well as Queen Elizabeth II and other members of the Royal Family.

In recent years Fayed was reported to say "he had the British Conservative government in the palm of his hand." In fact, in a scandal that rocked the government, involving some supposed dealings with Fayed, he insisted that "the British government was indeed for sale." Arab influence is being felt. Already, it has been reported that England has had to bow to their demand to allow them to divorce by saying "I divorce you," rather than through the conventional court process.

With the number of Muslim voters soaring, Islam is gaining a new and powerful influence in the United States.

Politics makes the United States
particularly vulnerable

The Washington Post, in an article titled, "Farrakhan presents dilemma for Clinton," said, "When State Department spokesman Nicholas Burns ... accused Mr. Farrakhan of "cavorting [with] dictators who have American blood on their hands, alarm bells sounded at the White House. A White House official called Mr. Burns to question his choice of words at the State Department's normally stolid briefing." The paper pointed out the political dangers for Mr. Clinton, "While the minister's views, seen by many as separatist and anti-Semitic, are offensive to many blacks, he commands the support of a large bloc of voters that Mr. Clinton can ill afford to alienate as he seeks a second term."

Even if Farrakhan broke the law, as he did when he took an offering in the Washington Mall, administration officials admit there are political problems in pursuing him — even if he has violated U.S. currency or foreign-agent registration laws. Moving against Farrakhan "could be perceived as moving against the black community," said Rep. Peter T. King, New York Republican. "They would probably like to get the job done, but do it in a very surgical way, where they don't get dragged into a fight with Farrakhan. Farrakhan's the type of guy (with whom) that's impossible."

The congressman said Mr. Clinton should unequivocally denounce Mr. Farrakhan's statements the same way he did when he publicly criticized rap singer Sister Souljah for racially divisive comments in 1992.

Newsweek magazine said White House political operatives called the State Department to head off a verbal sparring match with Mr. Farrakhan in an election year.

Farrakhan has caused political problems for President Clinton before. *The Washington Times* said, "In October, as he prepared to bring a huge crowd to Washington for the Million Man March, the White House debated what it should say. White House aides at first distanced the president from the march, but Mr. Clinton ended up endorsing the intent of the event — responsibility among black men — but not .

its leaders."[11]

    Americans need to answer this question, "If Farrakhan and the Arab-backed Muslims in America already have enough political clout to defy the laws of the United States today, what will they be doing tomorrow?

Chapter 3
The calypso singer who would be god

Like millions of other Americans I watched the news coverage of Louis Farrakhan and the Million Man March which attracted hundreds of thousands of black people to the mall in Washington, D.C. on October 16, 1995.

Black men of all ages, occupations, political persuasions and religions seeking a common commitment to strengthen the black family, gave new confidence to black youth, restored a sense of responsibility to black fathers and gathered in a commitment to improve.

The media gave the march the best possible headlines: "Throngs Hear Call for Solidarity of 'New Black Man'... A day of pride, prayer, song fills mall" (*The New York Times*). "Men Pledge New Start ... 400,000 vow to 'love my brother as myself'" (*USA Today*). "We Are Here to Rebuild' ... Farrakhan's message aims to awaken a nation torn by racial strife." (*The Rocky Mountain News*). We all wanted to believe this was true.

The great crowd made a wonderful pledge. "I pledge that from this day forward I will strive to love my brother as I love myself. I, from this day forward, will strive to improve myself spiritually, morally, mentally, socially, politically and economically for the benefit of myself, my family and my people...."

Despite the noble pledge and stated purpose, the Million Man March left some confused. *Newsweek* voiced an "uncertainty" about the results of the march: "In just two short weeks, the debate over race relations in America has shifted from the bitter aftermath of the O.J. trial to an anxious uncertainty left by the Million Man March."[1]

There was one clear-cut result from this, the largest black march in American history. Louis Farrakhan emerged as the new spiritual leader of black America. It was coronation day for a calypso singer with huge ambitions.

An Episcopalian from Roxbury

The boy that was to become the organizer of America's largest black march was born Louis Eugene Walcott in 1933 in the Bronx, N.Y. His mother was a domestic worker; his father was a school teacher and Baptist preacher. He grew up on Boston's Frederick Douglas Square, in Lower Roxbury. It was a thriving district of black-owned restaurants, nightclubs, and stores 50 years ago when Farrakhan was living there.

Louis attended St. Cyprian's Episcopal Church, the church of the West Indian immigrants. It was considered to be more sophisticated than the local Baptist church which was frequented by the "Homies." Louis's mother, strong-willed and deeply religious Mae Clark, had to raise her children alone, but she saw to it her two sons joined the congregation faithfully for Sunday services. Louis was described as "a devout Christian who sang in the choir, belonged to the youth fellowship, and was troubled by profanity."

Farrakhan says his mother, who immigrated from Barbados in 1920, paid for violin lessons. This resulted in his love for music. Farrakhan excelled in high school as a champion sprinter, a brilliant student, and as a calypso singer known as "the Charmer." After finishing high school he went to a teacher's college in Winston-Salem, N.C., on a track scholarship.

Outside Roxbury, Farrakhan was introduced to the grim realities of racism: being turned away from a theater in Washington D.C., and having to sit in the balcony of the church in North Carolina. "I saw the hypocrisy of the church claiming the love of Jesus Christ but practicing hatred," Farrakhan said. "I decided that I would start looking for a religion that would satisfy me. At that time in my maturity, I couldn't separate the sins of Christians from Christianity, from the true teachings of Jesus Christ."

After two years in college, he left for a career as a calypso singer. In 1952, back home in Boston, he was gripped by the preaching of a forceful ex-convict named Malcolm X. In 1955, he joined the Nation of Islam, serving as Malcolm's understudy. Overnight, the pious and polite Louis Walcott became Louis X and later Louis Abdul Farrakhan. The man who had once aspired to success in the white world, embraced black separatism, rejecting the white world as corrupt and degenerate. In 1957, the 24-year-old Farrakhan was appointed head of the old Mosque in Dorchester, when Malcolm transferred to Harlem.

When the leader of his Muslim denomination, Elijah Muhammad, died in 1975, his son began opening their organization to all Muslims. Because of this Farrakhan started publishing the *Final Call* newspaper and rallying "purists" to rebuild the organization. Farrakhan saw his opportunity and he seized it.

The Dangerous Ambition

From his very modest beginning Louis Farrakhan rose to become the most powerful black leader in America.

Naturally this success has changed him. Farrakhan with his colossal ego, and desire for personal gain and acclaim, now has "messiah aspirations." Martin Luther King, Jr. managed to maintain a semblance of humility that has escaped the boy from Lower Roxbury. He is a former calypso singer who would be god.

Farrakhan said he is the source of life for his people: "The voice of Elijah Muhammad coming through me is giving life to the entire Nation (of Islam). I warn you that when you turn me down and refuse this truth, you are turning down the Lord, the Savior, the Messiah, and the Deliverer that you seek."[2]

Farrakhan said if you revolt against him, you are revolting against "Almighty God." "You must remember my beloved Muslim brothers and sisters, the authority that Elijah Muhammad has today is divine He is from Almighty God, Allah, in person. Any minister who Elijah Muhammad appoints is appointed by divine authority; any laborer has divine authority; so when we revolt against this authority, set up by the divine, backed by the divine, we are actually revolting against God Himself."[3]

Farrakhan wears a ring that connects him to "god." In place of a wedding band, he flashes a giant gold ring emblazoned with 40 diamonds that form a silhouette of Elijah Muhammad. As the pope is wedded to Christ, Farrakhan says, "I am wedded to this man whom I believe is the Messiah." Pointing to the ring, he notes another detail – "a little tiny diamond where Mr. Muhammad's heart would be. I think that little, little-bitty diamond represents Farrakhan." If grandiloquence alone is enough to make a leader, then America will have to deal with Louis Farrakhan for a long time.

Farrakhan was introduced at his Chicago Saviors Day celebration with the words the prophet Isaiah used to introduce the coming Messiah, Jesus Christ, *For unto us a child is born, unto us a son is given: and the government shall be upon his shoulder: and his name shall be called Wonderful, Counsellor, The mighty God, The everlasting Father, The Prince of Peace* (Isaiah 9:6).

Farrakhan is undaunted by the fact that other black Muslim leaders ridicule the idea of him being divinely linked to God. W. Deen Mohammed, leader of the nation's largest African-American Muslim organization that claims 1.5 million followers while Farrakhan's group has an estimated 10,000 to 20,000, lashed out at his one-time colleague who he said is leading blacks "further and further into darkness." He said Farrakhan, "wants people to believe that God talks to him. If God is talking to him, I don't like what he is saying."

Silis Muhammad, leader of the "The Lost-Found Nation of Islam," a more militant faction, said, "Minister Farrakhan is an opportunist using Elijah's message to consolidate power only for himself." He called him ..."the Second Beast of the Book of Revelations."

It seems, as Louis Farrakhan demonstrates by his attitude, that the more recognition and status people acquire the more arrogant and certain they become of their judgment, or in his case, lack of judgment!

Such delusion of messianic expectations, also encourage self-appointed men of God to manipulate people to their own selfish ends. Farrakhan's ability to manipulate those who take him seriously is scary.

Farrakhan has the ability to draw gigantic crowds
Farrakhan's background as a musical entertainer

taught him to play to his audience and no one does this better. His ability to attract crowds and move crowds with his speaking talents has raised him to the heights of a legend. The power is not in the message, it is in the messenger and his ability to deliver it. That power has been astonishing.

A Farrakhan lecture outdrew the 1992 World Series on the same night. He filled the 16,500-seat Sports Arena in Los Angeles in October, 1994. Farrakhan drew 25,000 to the Jacob K. Javits Convention Center in New York in December of 1994.

But Farrakhan's crowning achievement was the Million Man March in Washington D.C. in October, 1995. The crowd estimates ranged from 400,000 to well over a million. A television producer told me he had filmed every march at the Capitol Mall dating back to Martin Luther King's rally there and this was the largest crowd he had seen. In addition to the crowd at the mall, some 2.2 million households were watching on television. Farrakhan's march was the highest-rated daytime speech in CNN history.

After so many years the black community had finally secured a new leader who could out-draw the historic rallies of Dr. Martin Luther King, Jr. Farrakhan reaches directly into the heart of what has become labeled the black "underclass" in ways no one else can even dream of doing.

He has the power to unify
bitterly diverse groups

Farrakhan has skillfully unified segments of three distinctly different black groups: The Nation of Islam, traditional Black Muslims and Black Christians. It is something of a miracle that three groups worshipping three different gods, with entirely different and even opposing beliefs could be brought together.

First, the Million Man March drew members of The Nation of Islam, which Farrakhan heads. They do not believe in a resurrection of the dead, an "unseen" god, or "spook" as Farrakhan labels Him. They believe Elijah Muhammad is god, Farrakhan is his prophet, there is no life after death and that it is God's will for them to set up a black kingdom on earth.

Farrakhan's second group of followers come from main stream Islam, from the Black Muslims. This group believes there is only one god Allah, Muhammad as the last prophet, life after death and that it is God's will for them to set up an inter-racial Islamic kingdom on earth.

His third group of followers, and the largest by far, come from Christian churches. This group believes there is only one god, Jehovah, Jesus was His incarnation, there is life after death and that it is not God's will for them to set up an earthly kingdom, but a heavenly one.

Farrakhan fills his sermons with quotes from Elijah Muhammad, the *Quran* and the *Bible* to appeal to all three groups. He has built an organization with leaders from all three. In his rallies, speakers from all three groups participate.

This strange and perverse union has been brought about by Farrakhan's oratory ability, his organizational skills and an angry discontent with the government of the United States.

A persuasive super-deceiver

Farrakhan demonstrates his tremendous persuasive powers by convincing his followers of bizarre things.

Space ships

Farrakhan has a fascination with space ships. He

teaches the message of Elijah Muhammad, that the black race moved to earth from outer space 66 trillion years ago.

Farrakhan says in 1985 he was taken aboard a space ship and beamed up to a Mother Wheel soaring 40 miles above the earth. On this space ship he met with Elijah Muhammad who told him Ronald Reagan was planning to invade Libya. Farrakhan warned Gadhafi as soon as he returned to earth.

He declares that someday a giant space ship is going to reign death down on all white people.

Louis Farrakhan even says there are 1,200 space ships following him around.

It would take a good persuader to sell these stories to the sanity board in a psychiatric hospital. Yet Farrakhan can sell them to millions of followers!

The crime stopper

Farrakhan has the persuasive power to convince his followers that the way to solve the crime problem is to put the Gestapo back on the streets, let all black criminals out of prison and send them back to Africa! Farrakhan points with pride to the fact he has cleaned-up drug and crime ridden ghettos. This has happened. One woman said she supported Farrakhan because he had run off the drug dealers, lowered crime and made her streets safe.

But, critics point to the fact that he uses strong arm techniques, and steps on human rights. Mussolini made the trains run on time. Hitler rid the streets of crime. But, the price the people paid in loss of personal freedom was far too high!

Farrakhan wants to release all black prisoners to a colony. Farrakhan told delegates to the African American

Summit '89 in New Orleans, La., "Let 'em go, let 'em do their time ... in Africa."[4]

The guide to prosperity

Nowhere is Farrakhan's ability to deceive the masses more evident than convincing his followers he can solve their money problems when he cannot solve his own. His social/economic message has proven most attractive to blacks. In 1985, he toured the United States speaking in cities and universities. Above him as he spoke was a banner declaring "POWER, AT LAST, FOREVER! MINISTER FARRAKHAN CALLS THE ENTIRE BLACK NATION TO ECONOMIC REBIRTH."[5]

Farrakhan brags about winning security contracts, starting companies and creating jobs. *Newsweek* magazine showed what a joke those claims are. His security enterprise is funded by the government and has a controversial record.[6] "The fact is he has yet to start a major business endeavor and has been a failure in many small ones."[7]

Farrakhan is a little confused. He says his mentor, Elijah Muhammad, is god and yet he directly disobeys Elijah's money policies. "I do not have to beg from our oppressor or march on their capitol with my hat in my hand, Muhammad wrote. "For how can I, on one hand, preach the doom of the oppressive system, and then with the other hand, ask alms of the oppressor?"[8]

Four months after the Million Man March, the organizers were struggling to raise $150,000 to pay off debts, but had not given any accounting of the money they collected. Joseph Certaine, a march organizer and Philadelphia's city government managing director finds these new fund raising appeals "troublesome" because the promise of a detail accounting of finances had been broken. No one knows how much money was raised. What is known is that every marcher was asked for an $11 donation prior to arriving in Washington D.C. Cash donations were collected at busy intersections from motorist arriving for the march. One thousand vending spaces were rented for as much as $1,000 apiece. Large cash contributions were collected as donation boxes were passed through the huge throng while Farrakhan spoke. Yet they need more money.

The most troublesome fact about the continued fund raising is the man doing it is the Rev. Benjamin F. Chavis, Jr., National director of the march. He was fired 18 months earlier as director of the NAACP after board members accused him of mishandling association finances.[9]

The Nation of Islam's financial empire is saddled with debt, failure and fraud allegations, but Farrakhan and his relatives live lavishly, according to a report in the *Chicago Tribune*. The IRS has filed more than $354,000 in liens against a Nation-linked security company, and is trying to collect $93,000 in taxes from a Nation-linked soap company the *Tribune* said. The Chicago building that Farrakhan calls his Sales and Office Building allegedly owes more than $1 million in property taxes.

Martin Luther King Jr.'s closest advisor, Stanley Levison, tells us that Martin talked about taking a vow of poverty, getting rid of everything he owned including his house - so that he could at least feel that nothing material came to him from his efforts. Farrakhan, in contrast, receives between $15,000 to $20,000 when he gives a speech.

The Bible clearly foretold the likes of Farrakhan, greedy prophets who would make "merchandise" out of their followers, *But there were false prophets also among the people, even as there shall be false teachers among you ... And through covetousness shall they with feigned words make merchandise of you* (2 Peter 2:1-3).

Farrakhan wins supreme dedication

Music moves people. A night of drum beating prepared ancient tribes to go out and die in battle. The music of Louis Farrakhan, this former calypso singer, is moving people to a fanatical dedication.

He can move his followers to dress different and act different. For him they will drive all the way to Washington D.C. and stand all day while he and his cohorts speak.

Farrakhan demands blacks, even policemen, not inform on other blacks, or side with the government against them. If they do this, it makes them a hypocrite and guarantees that Allah will burn them in the lowest depth of hell.

"When a Black Man who seeks the Truth and knows the Truth, willfully chooses to side with the enemy devil and become a hypocrite or an agent of the devil against his righteous brother, woe unto miserable hypocrite."

Farrakhan is successfully convincing black police they must stop arresting black men; black jurors must not vote against black criminals and Christians to stop following Jesus Christ. He demands and receives a higher allegiance to himself than to the government or the true God.

The future promises to
greatly increase Farrakhan's following

The future looks even better for Louis Farrakhan. People's expectations of prosperity are rising, while incomes of the uneducated blacks are declining in a new, high-tech world. This produces the kind of discontent Farrakhan can manipulate like a master. He identifies the cause of black distress as the "white devils" who oppress them. Farrakhan does this as effectively as Hitler blamed the Jews for the financial problems of the Germans in the depression of the 1930s. Farrakhan's one solution is to be free of the white man, either through a separate black state, a return to Africa, or the apocalyptic destruction of the white man.

The great American dream of prosperity: a good home, two fancy cars, a couple of TVs, designer clothes and exotic vacations for all Americans was always totally unrealistic. Robert Samuelson says, in his book *The Good Life and Its Discontents,* "the postwar boom bred an entitlement mentality which in turn bred disappointment and 'Good was no longer good enough'." George F. Will wrote, "As Lyndon Johnson said, it had to be a Great Society. And why not, John Kennedy having said, 'Man holds in his hands the power to abolish all forms of human poverty'." This idea stands in sharp contrast to Jesus' words, *Ye have the poor always with you* (Matthew 26:11).

In 1940, most Americans were renting their houses; the majority of homes did not have central heating or even electric lights, and only a tenth of the farm houses had a flush toilet. Only one American in 20 had a college degree, fifty years later one in five did. In 1964, there were fewer than 100 black elected officials nationwide compared to 7,000 in the 1990s. However, "good is no longer good enough" for a people sold on an impossible dream of prosperity for everyone. The longer people wait for their dream boat and the more consumer goods they see advertised, the more likely they are to believe Farrakhan.

Today the income of blacks is still only 60 per cent

that of whites. Black unemployment is double that of whites, 11 percent compared with 5 percent. Tragically, more than 60 percent of black families with children are headed by a single woman, giving little hope of them rising out of poverty.

The future promises an increase in the difference between income of the "haves and the have-nots." As their wage disparity grows Farrakhan's following should grow.

Jeremy Rifkin in his challenging book, *The End of Work*, says, "The wholesale substitution of machines for workers is going to force every nation to rethink the role of human beings in the social process ... Redefining opportunities and responsibilities for millions of people in a society absent of mass, formal employment is likely to be the single most pressing social issue of the coming century." It is certainly going to create a grave problem for America, where black unemployment is already soaring.

Rifkin concludes, "The end of work could spell a death sentence for civilization as we have come to know it." It is easy to imagine millions of blacks rioting and killing as the number of jobs continues to decrease and Farrakhan continues to blame it on the white man.

Many feel it is not for them to drive a beat-up Chevy while the white-collar worker is driving a "Caddy." To be realistic, people who do not want to develop a skill through a wearisome education process, or work much longer hours on a second job, or take the risk of starting a business of their own, cannot expect to have it all. But, Farrakhan skillfully stirs their dissatisfaction and tells them all they have to do is get rid of white men and their financial problems will be solved. As poverty grows, so grows Farrakhan's army of discontents.

Farrakhan has the power
to incite a Hitlerish hatred

While Farrakhan portrays himself to the media as a mild and moderate man he is becoming increasingly angry and much more radical. Farrakhan's hatred for the white government of the United States reached a new high in February, 1996, when he promised Muslim leaders the United States would be destroyed. He is infecting his followers with, a vicious hatred for America's white government and her white people.

Congressman Charles Rangel, who represents New York's Harlem district, has repeatedly stated that "the hatred spewed by Louis Farrakhan is scurrilous and intolerable."[10]

Wallace Deen Muhammad conducted a nationwide speaking tour during 1985 in an effort to counter Farrakhan's "rhetoric of hate."[11]

Carl T. Rowan, a black journalist who is among the highest respected men in his field, writes that Farrakhan "offers nothing more than religious bilge and racial hatred and is preying on the frustrations and rage of millions of black Americans."[12]

Al Neuharth, said in *USA Today* in an article titled, "The preaching of a prophet? Or just a devil's diatribe?," said Farrakhan's followers at the Million Man March, "reminded me of the Brownshirts who surrounded and seig-heiled Adolf Hitler at Nuremburg in 1934.[13]

Hitler: a "good" name
for a "great" man

Ironically, Farrakhan, in one of his rare compliments to a white person, called Adolph Hitler a "great" man: "The Jews don't like Farrakhan, so they call me Hitler. Well, that's

a good name. Hitler was a very great man."[14] He defend€
this with these words, "No, No. If what I have said is trut
then I can't back up from that ... If I said that Hitler was
wickedly great man, I spoke truth. I have nothing to aton
for....I cannot say to Jewish people if I speak the truth that I'r
sorry for speaking the truth. That's what prophets are sent t
do."

Curtis Turner, a business executive, said in the Bato₁
Rouge, La. *Morning Advocate*, "After watching the Loui₁
Farrakhan Million Man March ... one is left to wonder hov
everyone has failed to make a most poignant historica
connection with the Farrakhan gathering.

"One other man in recent history came to power with
an identical message. Adolf Hitler and Louis Farrakhan
conveyed a positive message almost identical in content. Both
espoused family values, self-reliance, better education, an
economic uplifting and a separatist state. Farrakhan and Hitler
also saw Jews as the "bloodsuckers" responsible for their
economic plight. ...I am sure if our liberal politicians and
press had been alive during Hitler's rise to power we would
have heard the same words being spoken by them about
Hitler's message ... 'separate the man from the message.'
Yes, the message is as good today as it was then. Germany
climbed out of economic ruin, built a great industrial state,
had virtually full employment, had an educated citizenry and
murdered 6 million Jews and as many Catholics, all in the
name of a great message.

"Farrakhan, standing on the podium, surrounded by his
black-uniformed 'jackbooted' thugs, cast an image far too
similar to that of Adolf Hitler.

"Can it happen again? Yes, it can...."[15]

Chapter 4
Dr. Martin Luther King Jr.'s
greatest enemy

It was a sad occasion when an assassin's bullet took away Dr. Martin Luther King Jr.'s life. Today, on a sadder occasion, another assassin is trying to take away all of Dr. King's achievements. Louis Farrakhan is dedicated to destroying everything Dr. King worked for.

Dr. Martin Luther King Jr., during his life, and for two decades after his assassination, set the direction for Afro-Americans. King had a conviction that all men were created equal and a dream that one day black and white children could sit down together. Dr. Farrakhan has a conviction that all men were created unequal and a dream that one day black and white children will be separated.

Dr. King was an integrationist who wanted blacks and whites to live together. Dr. Farrakhan is a separatist who wants blacks and whites to live separately.

Dr. King was a Christian who believed in a Bible that says love your enemies. Dr. Farrakhan is a Muslim who believes in a *Quran* that says fight those who do not believe in Allah and kill them when you can.

Dr. King believed in non-violence. Dr. Farrakhan believes violence is required.

In the 1960s Martin Luther King, Jr. raised Jewish

relations with blacks to a high with the vision of a "special relationship" between two long-suffering peoples supporting each other's freedom struggle. In the 1990s the relationship has reached rock bottom with the rise of Louis Farrakhan. Farrakhan calls Jews "bloodsuckers."

Dr. King improved race relations in America. Dr. Farrakhan is well on his way to destroying race relations in America.

Both men cannot be right, they are opposites.

Farrakhan is not only opposed to the policies of Dr. King, but also those of the most popular black man in American history, General Colin Powell. General Powell refused to attend the Million Man March because he did not wish to be seen as endorsing Louis Farrakhan.

Orlando Patterson wrote: "It is striking that many American separatists–Marcus Garvey, Malcolm X, Stokeley Carmichael, Louis Farrakhan have their roots in the West Indies. Because Caribbean blacks come from a richly diverse, majority black culture, once they find themselves in the minority here, they usually turn one of two ways Either they react militantly and struggle for separatism, or like Colin Powell, they strive hard for integration, trying to create a better version of the world from which they came." History tells us that the hope for black America lies with Colin Powell's way, not Farrakhan's.[1]

"Send the blacks back to Africa"

On April 23,1989, Farrakhan told delegates to the African American Summit '89 in New Orleans, La., that black prisoners in the United States needed to be transfered to a colony in their homeland of Africa: "Let 'em go, let 'em do their time ... in Africa."[2]

While visiting Africa in 1992, Farrakhan was reported to have looked at land that might serve as a colony for black prisoners in America.

When white men propose sending blacks back to Africa, crowds hiss. When Farrakhan proposes it, they applaud.

"White men were created by a black scientist"

The Nation of Islam incites racial hatred by teaching that white people were created by an evil black scientist. Elijah Muhammad said blacks belong to the tribe of Shabazz, which moved here from outer space 66 trillion years ago. The evil white race was created from all the evil in the universe by a black scientist named Yakub, 6,000 years ago. Blacks, as Allah's chosen people, will inherit the earth. He constantly reminded his people that they were not American's but members of an "Asiatic nation from the tribe of Shabazz."

Black Muslims are ordered to give up the "slave names" the white men gave to them and take a black Islamic name. Farrakhan doesn't bother to tell them these new names are actually white, Arab names.

The whites are plotting against the blacks

Farrakhan stirs black hate for whites by accusing whites of manufacturing AIDS and deliberately spreading it among blacks. He also blames the white govenment for making drugs easily accessible in poor, black neighborhoods in order to harm black people.

He blames white people for taking away the jobs of blacks: "America is losing her trade. ... Today, she's trying to tighten her belt. And to tighten her belt means to leave Black People out. Understand? You may have taken a day off fronl your job today, to show the power of Black Men in America as a working force, but I say to you, my beloved Black brothers and sisters, America is in such trouble today she cares not how long you strike. In fact, she's getting ready now to dump the Black Man off.[3]

Farrakhan says white people are to blame for blacks using dope and drinking alcohol: "Just remember what white America is doing when she floods the Black community with dope. The white man puts us in a ghetto, which is a playpen, and then you call yourself a "playboy". Just check yourself out, a bar on every corner, gambling, dope, everything that you need to keep your mind off of the serious business of NATION BUILDING."[4]

"Why are you a drunkard today, Black Man?" Farrakhan asks. "Because your enemy taught you to drink. He made the liquor, he sells the liquor, you buy it and get drunk off of it, and call it having a good time. He has made a fool out of you.[5]

The white man has corrupted the mind of black men, says Farrakhan: "Don't you know when a man puts his learning in you, he puts his way in you? ... So if the white man puts his intellect in you, his mind in you, you can't choose what is good for you. Invariably, you always choose what is good for your master. Therefore, for 400 years in America, no matter what we have done, it has always been to his good and to our detriment.[6]

Racism's super salesman

Mr. Farrakhan is not only America's No. 1 racist, he is very skilled at selling the radical racism that Dr. King and General Colin Powell fought against.

Farrakhan, doesn't deny his racism. He sells it; and

actually convinces audiences racism is a good thing: "Now today the [devil] has a new trick, for we have beaten back the hate propaganda and we have beaten back the Black Supremacy talk. Now he has a new propaganda technique. We're racists! (laugh) So now to the more modern brother, the more enlightened brother, he says, Well, I don't dig you Muslims. What's the matter, brother? Why don't you like us? We love you. He says, You're a racist. What do you mean racist? (Long pause) Ah! Now that you can't answer.

"If something is all Black...if a man wants to be with his own Black Self and his own Black Kind and love his own Black People and build for his own Black Self, is there something evil in that? No! Is it not natural for birds to be with their own kind? Black birds with black birds and white birds with white birds. Is it not natural for fish to swim in schools, each with their own kind? Is it not natural for you to love a member of your own kind? I don't feel bad when Jews love Jews. They're supposed to love each other. I don't feel bad when Italians love Italians. Well, don't you Jews and you Italians and you Greeks feel bad when a Black Man says he wants to love his own Black brother. That's none of your business!"

Farrakhan goes on to delight his audiences by proving racism is something to be proud of: "Look, if I play the violin and I give my life to the violin... I devote my time to the violin and I become a virtuoso at playing the violin... what do you call me? VIOLINIST! Umm! If I play the piano and I devote my life to the piano and I become a virtuoso at playing the piano...what do you call me? A PIANIST! And if I give my life to art and I practice my art day in and day out and I become skilled at it...what do you call me? ("ARTIST") Yeah! And if I want to give my life to my race, for my people, and devote my life and my energy to my people...what do you call me? (thunderous applause the ..."RACIST"!)[7]

Farrakhan said, "This evening, beloved brothers and sisters, when you ratify this 'Declaration of Black Independence,' you are one thousand and five percent right in that the black man of America must be independent from white America."[8]

Rep. Gary Franks of Connecticut said the Nation of Islam is the black equivalent of the Ku Klux Klan, "They are an organization that hides behind a veiled shield of doing what's good for their race while increasing the racial divide via their hatred for others."

Islam is a racist religion which teaches discrimination against Jews

Muslims have traditionally and skillfully used the hatred of which ever race is appropriate, in whatever country they are working. It is all rooted in the *Quran*. The *Quran* bitterly denounces "Jews" and "blacks." In the world where this book was written these were the two despised races. They made good scape-goats.

The *Quran* says Allah turned Jews into apes: "They had no Sabbath ...they were given to transgression ... a people whom Allah will destroy or visit with a terrible punishment .... They transgressed (all) prohibitions, we said to them: Be ye apes, despised and rejected" (*Quran* 7:163-166).

James Baldwin wrote in *The Harlem Ghetto*, "Just as society must have a scapegoat, so hatred must have a symbol. Georgia has the Negro and Harlem has the Jew."

Jews, apes and donkeys
In a classic example of religious racism the *Quran* says

the Jewish race is under a curse because they did not keep the Sabbath. This curse turned a whole community of Jews into "apes."

Islamic scholars say: "The punishment for breach of the Sabbath under the Mosaic law was death. ... There must have been ... a whole fishing community in a seaside town which persisted in breaking the Sabbath and were turned into apes."[9] Muslims seem to feel completely justified in whatever they do to mistreat Jews. If God curses them, why shouldn't Islam?

Again, the *Quran* likens Jews to "donkeys." It says, "The similitude of those who were entrusted with the Taurat (The Jews) ... is that of a donkey" (*Quran* 62:5).

When sports commentator Howard Cosell referred to an African American as a "monkey" during his broadcast of a 1983 NFL game. There was a widespread public outcry. Over 10 years later this was remembered in his obituaries. It appears there is a double standard at work. Call an African-American a "monkey" and you are in trouble. Call a Jew an "ape" and it goes unmentioned. You have to wonder why there is not a public outcry against Islam's *Quran*?

Farrakhan has continued in the Islamic tradition of Jew-bating. The Anti-Defamation League, a Jewish civil-rights group published this list of anti-Jewish statements Farrakhan made:

"We know that the Jews are the most organized, rich and powerful people, not only in America, but in the world. They're plotting against us even as we speak."[10]

"Some Jewish people in Hollywood put $30 million in Spike Lee's hands (to make the movie 'Malcolm X'). That's akin to 30 pieces of silver."[11]

"I'm not anti-Semitic, not a hater of Jews and whites.

It's not your complexions or your faith that has messed up the world. It's the way you think."[12]

The Quran targets Jews
for Muslim attacks

Jews and Christians who do not embrace Islam are mentioned specifically as targets of Islamic attack: "Fight against such of those to whom the Scriptures were given as believe neither in Allah nor the Last Day, who do not forbid what Allah and His apostle have forbidden, and do not embrace the true faith until they pay tribute out of hand and are utterly subdued" (*Quran*, 9:29). According to the Muslims, Jews and Christians knew the truth, but "they worship their rabbis and their monks, and the Messiah the son of Mary, as gods besides Allah; though they were ordered to serve one God only. There is no god but Him" (*Quran* 9:31).

History documents the way in which Islam has stirred hatred for Jews and led Muslims into wars against the Jews.

Muslims continually stir whites against blacks in Islamic countries and blacks against whites in the United States, but they universally vent their hatred for Jews. Like Adolph Hitler, Farrakhan blames the Jews for problems in the black community.

When the Nation of Islam-run company lost its contract for public housing security in Baltimore, they blamed it on the Jews. Abdul Arif Muhammad, spokesman for the company said, "HUD has been forced into a situation. They have capitulated to the pressure of the American Jewish League and the American Jewish Congress." The truth is Wells Fargo Security submitted the lowest bid last year and was awarded the contract. It had nothing to do with the Jews.[13]

Nowhere is the difference between Dr. King and Dr. Louis Farrakhan more evident than in their attitude toward Jews. Countless Jewish organizations have raised and given millions of dollars to support the goals of the black race. B'nai B'rith, a prominent social-action organization, undertook, on behalf of the Jewish people, many of the activities that Dr. King had asked the United States government to perform for Negroes. This organization is financed by Jewish charities and private donations.

Dr. King admitted that the Negro civil rights groups, including his own, were in financial straits and relied heavily on white philanthropy, particularly from the Jews who have had an enormous investment in their relations with the black community, and have for so long a time been the most visible and generous non-black allies of the civil rights movement.

He always said that the Jewish race would have a special place in his heart and his prayers and would forever thank them for their unwavering strength and support. "They are a people who understand oppression," he preached. "And without any hesitation or fear for their own safety, they marched side by side with me for justice."

Farrakhan's anti-Semiticism

In November of 1995 the Nation of Islam spewed out its hatred for Jews. Farrakhan's top aide, Khallid Abdul Muhammad, made a vicious speech against the Jews at New Jersey's Kean College. Farrakhan merely gave him a slap on the wrist for his "mockery". He said he could not disavow the Anti-Semitic, anti-Catholic 'truths' his aide had spoken.

Michael C. Kotzin, Director of the Jewish Community Relations Council of the Jewish United Fund of Metropolitan Chicago, said "that the problem with Farrakhan is not that he and his followers 'occasionally' come out with vicious anti-semitic comments; these comments are just the tip of the iceberg, revealing not just an intense hostility towards the Jewish people but an ideology that is anti-semitic at its core."

Kotzin goes on to say "that Farrakhan is driven by a belief system which sees Jewish villainy, Jewish conspiracies and Jewish control everywhere. He teaches a complex theology which sees him and his followers as the true Jews as chosen people who have suffered 400 years of slavery. It is he who has been chosen by God to take them out of oppression."[14]

Islam teaches
a black women is an evil sign

Muhammad, the founder of Islam, declared that a black woman was an evil omen. The *Hadith* says Muhammad thought a dream of a black woman was an evil omen, signaling a coming epidemic of disease (*Hadith* vol. 9, nos. 162, 163). Combining two favorite Islamic prejudices against women and blacks, Muhammad preached that they were under a curse. Playing to the worst possible fears, he said a black woman was the sign of a plague. It was taught to fear a black woman as you would a deadly epidemic, to see one was to be a victim of the other.

Omens play well in the minds of those who do not know God's truth. They are impressed with stories of dreams, particularly when they agree with the racial bias of the listeners. The Bible says, *The prophet that hath a dream, let him tell a dream; and he that hath my word, let him speak my word faithfully. What is the chaff to the wheat? saith the Lord* (Jeremiah 23:28). Muhammad had a racist dream about blacks and made it a part of his Islamic religion.

Islam's leaders call black people "ugly"

Islam runs down black people. Muslim scholar Malik Ibn Ons, in referring to the control Muhammad gave Muslims over their slaves, said: "The master does not have the right to force the female slave to wed to an ugly black slave."[15]

Another Islamic leader used the same word, "ugly," in explaining Islam's position on slaves: "The master has the right to force his male or female slave to marry without obtaining their approval."[16] But after agreeing with this right to force two slaves to marry, Malik Ibn Ons made an exception. The slave owner cannot make a slave woman marry "an ugly black slave."

So, slavery is approved and forcing slaves to marry is alright, as long as you do not force a female slave to marry "an ugly black slave."

The exemption here is plainly because of color, not other features. The text does not say you cannot force slaves to marry ugly "white" people. The word ugly clearly refers to the black skin color. To Muhammad, and the founding fathers of Islam, black people were ugly.

America's Black Muslims have no problems with the Islamic hatred for Jews. What is a problem is the historic discrimination, hatred for and enslavement of black people.

In the Arab world where blacks are despised, the Arabic version of the *Quran* is naturally the preferred version. It says, "Only men with white faces will be saved" (*Quran* 3:106, 107). "On the Day of Resurrection you shall see their faces blackened, those who uttered falsehoods about God" (*Quran* 39:60)? It does something even the Ku Klux Klan never did – assign people to hell on the basis of their skin color.

Obviously this teaching would create a problem in converting black people to Islam. So in order to appeal to and deceive blacks, they have put out an English version of the *Quran* which inserts the words to make it read: white "light upon their" faces. They take advantage of the fact that blacks in the United States and in Africa cannot read the original Arabic, and do not understand that the original book, written in the "heavenly language" of Arabic says they cannot ever go to heaven because of their skin color. Islam skillfully goes whichever way the wind of racism flows by appealing to the lowest elements of human nature.

What a contrast this is to the Bible which Farrakhan left to embrace Islam. It commands us not to look at the outward appearance of a person, but to look at the heart, the character of the inner person, as God does. "But the LORD said unto Samuel, Look not on his countenance, ... for the LORD seeth not as man seeth; for man looketh on the outward appearance, but the LORD looketh on the heart" (1 Samuel 16:7).

Muhammad owned black slaves

One of the Nation of Islam's top recruiting tools has always been to graphically describe the horrors of the slave trade. Farrakhan tells about the millions of blacks who died on the voyage over here, and how the black women were raped and killed by the "white, Christian slave traders." He accuses the Jews of being the major traffickers in early American slave trading.

Farrakhan stirs his followers with gory tales of black slaves suffering in America. He blames this on the "Jews" and "the white men." American Muslims deceitfully covers up is the fact that the prophet Muhammad had black slaves, that

Muslims have sold black slaves for 1,400 years and that Muslims are the only people in the world who are still selling blacks into chattel slavery today.

The greatest scholar of Islam, Ibn Qayyim al-Jawziyya, said in his book, *Zad al-Ma'ad*, "Muhammad had many male and female slaves. He used to buy and sell them, but he purchased (more slaves) than he sold, especially after God empowered him by His message ... He (once) sold one black slave for two. His name was Jacob al-Mudbir." (Ibn Qayyim al-Jawziyya, *Zad al-Ma'ad*, Part I, p.160)

The *Hadith* says, "When visiting the home of Muhammad, Umar bin Al-Khattab found that 'a black slave of Allah's apostle was sitting on the first step.'" (*Hadith* vol. 6, no. 435)

It is a hard fact for American Muslims to deal with, but the founder of Islam, Muhammad, owned black slaves.

Islam was the major trader
in American black slavery

While Farrakhan is propagating the outlandish tale that Jews were the major sellers of black slaves in the American colonies, the well-documented fact is Islam was the major seller of blacks. Jews had almost no part whatever in it. Islam was the major player.

African historian J.E. Inikori says between 650 and 1900 Arab slave-traders drained Black Africa of 14.4 million people

The Nation of Islam has published this amusing statement: "Jewish slave traders procured Black Africans by the tens of thousands and funneled them to the plantations of South America and throughout the Caribbean ... In fact, in all the American colonies ... Jewish merchants frequently dominated."[17]

Dr. Harold Brackman, in his well cocumented book, *Ministry of Lies* wrote: "The truth is Jewish traders dealt in pagan white slaves from Slavic areas, but never played a predominant role and ceased to be involved around the year 1000 AD, 500 years before the first enslaved Africans were carried to the New World."[18]

Blackman said, "Between the years 650 and 1900, ten million or more Black Africans were carried by slavers either north across the Sahara or east over the Red Sea/Indian Ocean route. This trade was in the hands, not of Jews, but of Muslim merchants who made 'Arab' synonymous with 'slaver' and also supplied the Atlantic slave traffic."[19]

Yale professor David B. Davis says, "The Arabs and their Muslim allies were the first people to develop a specialized, long-distance slave trade from sub-Saharan Africa. They were also the first people to view Blacks as suited by nature for the lowest and most degrading form of bondage."[20]

Farrakhan's Nation of Islam not only lied about the Jewish role in American slavery, they have concocted some preposterous story about 200 million blacks dying as a result of American slavery of blacks and blamed the Jews for this "holocaust." At a community forum promoting their book, *The Secret Relationship*, a spokesman from the Nation of Islam said, "we lost more than 200 million during the Middle passage alone." All the available merchant ships could not have carried over 20 million from Africa during that time frame.

Thorough historical studies now give an estimate of between eleven million and nineteen million deaths before, during, and after the Middle Passage to America. This is a terrible figure, but it is only a fraction of the deaths Farrakhan is claiming. And it must be remembered that Muslims played the major role in these deaths.

The Islamic tradition of
selling black slaves continues today

The May 4, 1992, edition of *Newsweek* documents Islam's enslavement of blacks, even showing pictures: "The Islamic Republic of Mauritania finds it easier to lie about slavery than to abolish it. ... More than 100,000 descendants of Africans conquered by Arabs during the 12th century are still ...living as old-fashioned chattel slaves." *Newsweek* says slavery is making a comeback in Sudan, "once virtually rid of slavery ... The government counter-insurgency strategy has included arming the Arab tribespeople ... The result has been a resurgence of traditional raiding, including slave taking. .... The slaves are Filipinos, Indians, Pakistanis, Bangladeshis and West Africans."[21]

The Economist says, "In Sudan, chattel slavery is spreading fast, as a consequence of the civil war between the black Christians ... and the Arab, Muslim north."[22]

Jean Sassion, a Saudi Princess, shocked the Muslim world in 1992 with her book documenting that her Islamic family had many black slaves. On page 29 of the *Princess* she writes, "We owned a family of Sudanese slaves. Our slave population increased each year when Father returned from Kaj, the annual pilgrimage to Mecca made by Muslims, with new slave children."

This pious Muslim made his holy pilgrimage to Mecca to worship Allah and returned home with black Sudanese slaves.

Islam is a "white man's religion" contrary to Farrakhan's distortions

Muslims in the United States tell African-Americans that Christianity is the white man's religion and Islam is "the black man's religion." The truth is the Islamic faith and America's Nation of Islam were started by "white" men. Four times the *Hadith*, compiled by Dr. Muhammad Muhsin Khan and recognized by all Muslim authorities, says the Prophet Muhammad was "white."

The *Hadith* says: "a man came ... and then said, 'Who amongst you is Muhammad?' ... We replied, 'This white man reclining on his arm" (*Hadith* vol. 1, no. 63).

Muhammad is referred to as "a white person" in the *Hadith*. (*Hadith* vol. 2, no. 122). The *Hadith* says when Muhammad raised his arms, "the whiteness of his armpits became visible" (*Hadith* vol. 2, no. 141). Again, Anas "saw the whiteness of the penis of Allah's Prophet" (*Hadith* vol. 1, no. 367).

Minister Fard, the founder of Farrakhan's Nation of Islam, was a white man. Ironically, he conceived the doctrines that the white man was the "devil" and the black man was superior, before he mysteriously "disappeared."

Arthur Magida, who is writing an unauthorized biography on Farrakhan, said, "He's been trying to prove his blackness to himself and others all his life." Farrakhan was conceived in an affair. His mother was afraid the baby would be light and advertise her unfaithfulness. She tried to abort herself three times with a coat hanger, but failed.[23] This raises questions about how "black" Louis Farrakhan is.

Will we perish as fools?

W. Deen Mohammad, leader of the nation's largest

African-American Muslim organization, said, "Louis Farrakhan is leading blacks further and further into darkness."

"Racial polarization is emerging as a major national problem; and if current trends persist, the United States faces an unraveling that could make the Soviet Union's dissolution look tame by comparison, says the *Utne Reader*. "The pace of polarization is quickening... Among the troubling portents ... the mushrooming popularity of Black Muslim leader Louis Farrakhan and his notions of racial separation. If the politics of polarization continue unabated, the country will suffer irreparable damage. Not only are working-class whites rejecting civil rights goals, but African-American youth increasingly are rejecting the idea of racial reconciliation."[24]

Dr. Martin Luther King, Jr. said, "We must learn to live together as brothers or we will perish as fools."

62

Chapter 5
The beginning of
the second civil war

"Oh, Washington, D.C.; oh, government of America; you shall pay well for your evil ... there is a God on the scene ... and He's anxious to kill you," warned Louis Farrakhan. "He's anxious to destroy you. ... So rush on with your plan, and rush on to your death," declared the Muslim leader. "This, my beloved Black brothers and sisters ... is the end of the white man's power to rule and dominate the lives of Black people ... This is the beginning of their sorrows."[1]

The racial revolution Farrakhan proposses has failed to alarm American's in large numbers. The country is in a state of denial, reluctant to admit racial war could happen and refusing to admit how horrible it would be.

As the Muslim minister fanned the racial fires it took me back in memory to the 1992 race riot in Los Angeles. My wife and I could never have imagined such a devastating scene if we had not been there. For two days we drove through the ruins of what had once been the dream city of Los Angeles. It was burning proof that racial war can happen in the U. S. It was vivid evidence of how horrible it can be for everyone involved.

Following the juries announcement of "not guilty" for the

policemen that had beaten Rodney King, an ominous cloud had settled over the tropical city. The L.A. Lakers canceled their playoff game. After three years of playing to packed crowds, the Phantom of the Opera play was shut down. Andrew Hacker's compelling book, *Two Nations: Black and White, Separate, Hostile, Unequal,* was selling in the bookstores. On the radio, Rapper Ice Cube was singing, "pay respect to the black fist, or we'll burn your store right down to a crisp."

Simmering close to the surface, undetected or more likely denied by the majority; the time bomb had been armed and ready to blow. "For more than a year he had been a writhing body, twisting on the ground under kicks and nightstick blows in what may be the most endlessly replayed video tape ever made (the tape of the police beating Rodney King)." [2]

This graphic horror of police brutality was the fuse. It should have come as no surprise, when the King verdict was handed down by a mostly white Simi Valley jury with its large population of policemen, that it would cause a racial bomb to detonate; sending deadly, fearful fallout throughout this nation.

Deep-seated hatred, ultimately fueled by the King verdict had driven hundreds in. this city into a kind of temporary "insanity."

A night of hell

David Johnson, a union organizer, was driving through downtown Los Angeles on the Santa Ana Freeway. Normally at that time of day the freeway would be jammed with cars. Now he could see only three or four. There was something even more startling: a setting sun burning red through huge clouds of black smoke. All over the city, pillars of smoke billowed. Overhead, the sky turned red with the reflection of burning buildings. The acrid smell burned his nostrils. This was not some fantasy production of Universal Films. This was horrifyingly real. The race rioters had turned this land of beautiful movie myths into an ugly, frightening reality.

Over the car radio streamed frantic, near-hysterical news reports. They switched from scene to scene to give details of casualties. It was like being in a war zone, Johnson thought. Fearfully, the white union organizer, found himself glancing from side to side looking for snipers on street corners.

Elder Hwang, a Korean-American merchant, who had arrived in the United States in 1964 and earned a master's degree in business, grew alarmed. Closing his dry cleaning business he stepped out into a mob of more than a hundred people. Two shots were fired at him; he could feel a burning where a bullet singed his right arm. Hwang escaped from the mob, his store did not; it was looted and burned. His whole life's work was gone. He had no insurance. Hwang felt a murderous rage; his initial reaction was to seek revenge, to knock down and kill blacks.

By Friday morning 90 percent of the Korean-owned stores, and markets in South Central L.A. had been wiped out. The Koreans suffered damage or destruction to almost 2,000 stores.... Koreans were enraged when a woman wrote a newspaper column saying that the Korean community equated the life of a black child with the cost of a $11.59 bottle of orange juice.

The black rapper "Ice Cube," added to the tensions with a song that Koreans took as a summons for blacks to kill Korean merchants. Entitled "Black Korea," it's lyrics offer a glimpse into the resentments and hatreds among African-Americans in the inner cities who feel humiliated by the treatment they receive from "Oriental, penny-countin' motha f----- storekeepers." The final verse concludes ominously and foreshadows what took place during the riots with a warning about respecting "the black fist" and burning the Korean markets "to a crisp."

"It was the only time since I came to America that I was afraid. There are times now when I am driving to church, so many people are scared to death," said Paul John, the Korean owner of a Christian bookstore. He was speaking to me from in front of his business as we looked out at the devastation of the riots. Paul John was obviously terrified as he related how close he had come to losing his business, and his life.

The Koreans had their own grievances. Their community had been subjected to numerous killings by blacks – thirty-two such homicides between 1988 and 1991. But they had controlled their anger.

Most of the destruction was in a 46 square mile part of South Central L.A. that is plagued by crime, gangs, poverty, and drug dealers. This is a breeding ground that spawns racism and separatism, the integral part of the hate doctrine preached by the Nation of Islam's Louis Farrakhan.

In the aftermath of the rioting, *Time* magazine's George J. Church wrote, "It had not exactly been unknown that race relations were worsening, a hundred voices said so. But not until last week did many whites and blacks realize how deep an abyss had been opening at their feet. And last week's violence is all too likely to make the gulf still wider and deeper."[3] *Time's* David Ellis wrote, "Not surprisingly, it was the besieged black community that suffered the most. In a bid to protect their businesses from the rioter's wrath, a number of shopkeepers desperately posted signs declaring that their stores were BLACK OWNED. In most cases, the signs were ignored by looters and arsonists who destroyed the stores anyway.[4]

A commentator said, "The City of Angels turned into the dwelling of demons."[5] An urban nightmare became an immediate grim reality and violent hatred ruled the streets of Los Angeles for two whole days; a hatred and destruction that repeated itself, albeit to a lesser degree, in San Francisco, Atlanta, Seattle, Pittsburgh and many more of our American cities.

On Friday afternoon Rodney King went before the T.V. cameras and pleaded for the violence to stop. "Stop making it horrible, he muttered, "just not right ... just not right." His plea was to no avail.

Newsweek gave this description of the worst riot in American history: "Streets swarming with defiant youths, whole city blocks on fire, looters streaming out of stores with anything they could carry; these were images that the nation hadn't seen for years and had hoped never to see again."

An eyewitness to the riots said, "You are looking at an enormous fire here and at the same time there is another fire just around the corner and one up the street; the police and the fire department just racing up and down the street. There were not nearly enough fire fighters in the city to control this number of fires. Many of the firemen that did come to help were driven away by snipers firing at them."

In 1967, forty-three people were killed in Detroit, thirty-four in Los Angeles, in a replay of the Watts riots there two years earlier, and twenty-six died in Newark, but property damage, though extensive in all these riots, did not come close to L.A. in 1992.

Time magazine reported "whites and blacks have actually more in common than they think: the dominant thinking is that both condemn the acquittal and the rioting. If these are the thoughts then why can't we extend our hands and reach out to our brothers and sisters and by these actions unite the United States of America'?"

In an article entitled "The Trashing of Los Angeles," Kermit Lansner wrote, "A quarter of a century after the vast racial conflagrations in Watts, and Detroit and Washington, and dozens of other cities throughout the country, the nation watched aghast as a paroxysm of violence and terror engulfed Los Angeles. When it was over, it should be pointed out, there were more casualties ... than the U.S. suffered in the Gulf War."[6]

It was a "night of hell."

A preview of Civil War II

As the anger and bloodshed in Los Angeles spilled uncontrollably out of the television screens, millions of Americans feared that this terrible unrest would spread to their own cities. As one police official told me "their fear is fully justified; all the major cities in America are powder kegs, that are ready to explode into racial riots like this and worse."

While seventeen thousand murderers and arsonists ravaged Los Angeles, one commentator said, "We are looking at what could be the beginning of the Second Civil War." Despite riots around the country, the riots did not start such a war, but it gave Los Angeles a preview of what it would be like.

Is it difficult to even imagine an army of arsonist and

snipers rampaging all across America? The Los Angeles riots destroyed a billion dollars worth of property, killed 60, injured 2,000 and spread terror through the city. How many would have to die if such rioting ever spread across the nation?

It is difficult to even think what it would do to our economy. The Los Angeles riots left 40,000 people out of work. Some parts of the city virtually ceased to function. Many of the businesses were never rebuilt. A black victim of the riots told me, "They looted a lot of mini-marts and burned down a lot of stores. And I lost my job. It's hard to find a job in L.A. right now." Los Angeles has had to declare bankruptcy.

Billy J. Tidwell, a social scientist at the National Urban League in Washington D.C. reckons our ethnic problems are already costing us $93 billion a year. Imagine what a race war would do to the economy. Edward D. Irons, Dean of Business at Clark Atlanta University in Atlanta, said, "Unless we get a handle on racism, foreign competitors are going to eat us for lunch."

Just think of what it could mean to America's educational system. The riots in Los Angeles shut down the schools. The children were sent home. Los Angeles stopped educating children and started shooting them.

Racism has the potential of devastating our judicial system as it did Los Angeles'. Police become the targets for snipers. Juries weigh every case concerning race on the basis of will my vote mean my home will be burned and my family shot? Every one in Los Angeles has to wonder, "If I was on a jury that gives a guilty verdict to a black person, what will happen to my home - to my family? Or if I find a policeman guilty, will I lose my protection?"

Henry Louis Gates, the chairman of Afro-American

studies at Harvard stated: "that (King) jury was more afraid of the potential of being mugged by some hypothetical black male than it was of the abuse of the Constitution of civil rights." Will racism force us to abandon the liberties of our constitution for the protection of a police state?

John Dickinson wrote, in his 1768 *Liberty Song*, "…. Then join in hand, brave Americans all! By uniting we stand, by dividing we fall."   With Farrakhan and the Muslim keeping up their message of racial hate and the dividing gap between the races growing, we must stop and consider the possibility of the Republic falling.

Nineteen hundred years ago, Jesus Christ said, a house divided against itself cannot stand.   Los Angeles forced Americans to see their nation as a divided nation.   It also forced them to wonder how much longer their divided nation can stand. The Bible prophesied that in the last days divided, violent, hate-filled people would plunge the world into an international Armageddon. Such violent, hate-filled people are already threatening to plunge the United States into an American Armageddon.

In the ashes of Los Angeles, America could have received her last warnings.

Preparing for the coming fiery trial

The Apostle Peter wrote to Christians just several months before they were to enter a time of great suffering and told them to prepare for the "fiery trials" that were to come upon them: *Beloved, think it not strange concerning the fiery trial which is to try you, as though some strange thing happened unto you: ….* (1 Peter 4:12-16).

Racial hatred has already brought a terrible fiery trial upon the people of Los Angeles. It could bring one on the entire United States. It is time for us to face the possibility and prepare.

The majority of people say, when asked, that they were caught unaware by the Los Angeles riots, but they should certainly not have been surprised. We are living is a wicked and violent world where Satan is the god of this age. God has forewarned us of the wickedness that will come. We must be prepared for whatever our future holds.

A second civil war is a possibility. Beset by real economic fears and chaos of the inner city, many black people are starving for Farrakhan's rhetoric of "going it alone." He preaches black self-help but covers it with the cloak of racism. He uses the teachings of the *Quran*, which advocates violence and death to anyone who does not claim Allah as his God. To this end he stirs the boiling cauldron, laced with his lethal doses of hate, perversion of the truth and separatism.

So many impoverished black people are so hungry for the message that they choose to ignore its dangers. Farrakhan's timing is good: the black community, nurtured in the church-based civil rights movement is divided, confused and exhausted by their community's pleas for answers.

When Louis Farrakhan speaks, I cannot help but remember the riot-torn city of Los Angeles. As he raves of revolution, of the end of the white man's rule, and of the final death and doom that must come to every white person; it conjures up such horrific memories. I cannot help but wonder if the Los Angeles riots were a preview of what is coming for America.

Chapter 6
To kill and die for sex

Mrs. Hillary Rodham Clinton made history on February 20, 1996 when she held the first Islamic religious event at the White House. She played host to 150 people, including several Muslim families and army Chaplain Abdul-Rasheed Muhammad, the first Islamic chaplain in the U.S. military. The first lady praised Islam for being, "the fastest growing religion in America," and referred to the reception as an "historic and overdue occasion." Mrs. Clinton gave her daughter Chelsea, who had taken a course in Islamic history, credit for teaching her about the Muslim religion.

Mrs. Clinton's religious event coincided with the end of Ramadan, when Muslims have a feast after 30 days of fasting, gather at Mosques for morning prayers and visit cemeteries.

"A greater understanding of the tenets of Islam in our national consciousness will help us build strength and resilience as a nation," Mrs. Clinton told the group. "The values that lie at the heart of Ramadan – faith, family, community and responsibility to the less fortunate - resonate with all the peoples of this Earth."

Chaplain Muhammad read from the *Quran* and then presented Mrs. Clinton with a copy of the book. If she ever has time to read this book she is going to find it very surprising. The religion she praised for its "family" values teaches a man is to beat his wife, marry up to four women, divorce them by saying the words, "I divorce you," and uses them as bait to get Muslims to fight and die for Allah.

Most Americans are shocked when they are forced to face the truth about sexual relations in the Muslim world. I remember our surprise when my wife and I met a Muslim on the barren plains of Israel's wilderness who had four wives, the *Quran's* quota. He invited us to have tea with him at his tent home. One of his wives prepared the tea and brought it out of the tent and sat it on the ground some distance from us. The husband went over, picked it up and proceeded to serve us. Later, an Israeli friend explained her husband forbid her to serve, or have any contact with a man other than himself. His control of his wives was as surprising as the number of them.

Years later, my wife and I were visiting an Islamic country, when a Muslim walked up to a friend who was traveling with us and offered him three camels for his wife. My first reaction was to laugh over how indignant she was that he did not think she was worth more than three camels. Later she learned that this was an extremely generous offer for a wife in a Muslim country.

In 1994, I sat on the floor of America's largest Mosque, in New York's upper Manhattan Island and asked the Iman, their top teacher, about Islam's practice of taking multiple wives. He explained, "In America a man marries a woman, and in a few years he becomes tired of her. He sees another woman he likes and has an affair." The Iman explained, "In Islam, when a man sees another woman he likes, he marries her." "But," he said, "in Islam we are very, very moral with our wives. If you give one a present you must give all the wives a present. If you sleep a night with one wife, you must sleep one night with the other wives."

Like Mrs. Clinton, I was given a copy of the *Quran*. When I started reading it, I was as shocked as most people raised in the Christian faith would be. It made me realize what a bizarre role women play in the Muslim's religion. From the beginning of the Islamic revolution Muhammad understood what a powerful force sex was in the Islamic revolution. He found sex could provide him with three vital essentials in his conquests.

Sex a recruiting tool for revolutionaries

Farrakhan, like Muhammad before him, is using sex as a powerful recruiting tool to build a large Islamic army. What could be more attractive to the average man than the Islamic offer of all the sex he wants with a variety of women he has absolute control over and doing it with the approval of god?

Whatever Farrakhan may say about family values, he teaches a sexist religion that is geared to the pleasure of men for it is men that fight in revolutions.

Farrakhan's *Quran* allows a man to have four wives, if he is able to "deal justly," or take care of all of them. This prevents him from "doing injustice," or having an affair with another Muslim's wife. This book Muslims are taught was authored by Allah says, "Marry women of your choice, Two or three or four; but if ye fear that ye shall not be able to deal justly (with them), then only one, or (a captive) that your right hands possess, that will be more suitable, to prevent you from doing injustice" (*Quran* 4.03, Yusufali translation).

The *Quran* forbids a Muslim to engage in sex with another man's wife except in the case of his married slave women: "All married women (are forbidden unto you) save those (captives) whom your right hands possess. It is a decree of Allah for you" (*Quran* 4:24, Pickthal translation).

The *Quran* does not restrict men from having sex with just four women, just four wives. Allah is "cognizant" of a man's sexual appetite. If he finds slave girls whose beauty pleases him he may have as many as he wants. The *Quran* says the slave girls do not count towards his limit of four: "It shall be unlawful for you to take more wives ... though their beauty please you, except where slave-girls are concerned. God takes cognizance of all things" (*Quran* 33:52, Dawood translation).

Muslim historians tell us Muhammad was intrigued with brutalizing women and having sex with children. He once married a six-year-old. "How miserable women are in Muhammad's view, he orders men to scourge them, forces young virgins to marry against their will (Muhammad himself took Aisha, at six years of age; the difference in their ages was forty-five years. Muhammad at that time was fifty-four, the age of her grandfather). A father may give his consent to have his young virgin daughter married without obtaining her permission....he took his daughter Aisha, when she was six years old and married her to the prophet Muhammad without her permission."[1]

The sixties sex revolution brought public approval to many sex partners. The Islamic revolution brings a divine approval to many sex partners.

This is awkward for Farrakhan to deal with these teachings of Islam while living in a Christian concept of loyalty to one woman. But he cannot deny Allah allows men to have sex with many women. The *Quran* is clear on this point. Some effectively deal with this by merely hiding this teaching. This is easily done because many do not understand the *Quran*. Others, like the New York Iman, rationalize that it is better to marry an extra woman than to merely have an affair with her. He doesn't mention the slave girls, the *Quran* allows a man to have sex with.

While some Muslims defiantly deny this and others rationalize it by saying two or three wives are better than two or three affairs, the facts are there for all to read. The *Quran* reduces a woman to a sexual toy for a man. And all Muslims believe their *Quran* is the infallible word of God. The growth of Islam in America has to be attributed to men. And a great part of the religion's attraction to Islam has to be attributed to the appeal of divine approval of promiscuous sexual pleasures. Muslims offer a religion that unbridles young men from the Christian standard of faithfulness to one wife. This makes Islam a lot more attractive than Christianity to licentious young men who are more interested in gratifying their passions than in gratifying the needs of a woman, much less the needs of a holy God.

A friend of mine was brought face to face with the Muslim sexual practices which is so attractive to men and so deplorable to women. She told me that thirty years ago in England she had a very beautiful female cousin, whose name was Sylvia. She said: "Sylvia was ten years older than I; I always admired her and wanted to be like her; she had beautiful blonde hair, blue eyes and a peach complexion. She was always full of life and had an unquenchable thirst for adventure. When she was eighteen she went on a vacation to the Middle East. On this vacation she met a handsome Lebanese Sheik and fell in love. She told her parents that she was going to marry him, but they were very afraid for her; they said they had heard stories that Muslim men had many wives and harems full of concubines. They had heard that the wives were kept as virtual prisoners with very few rights. They also had heard that Middle Eastern men coveted the blonde hair and blue eyes of a European woman; it was like a trophy.

"Sylvia told them not to be afraid; her future husband was a very modern Muslim and did not think and behave like that. She also told them that he had said "he would never take another wife, as with Sylvia he only needed the one." Sylvia was married in a small civil ceremony in London with her parents in attendance and then taken by her husband back to Lebanon, where she converted to Islam and was married in an Islamic ceremony.

"She seemed to be happy for a few years and had two handsome sons. Then without any warning, her parents did not hear from her for quite a few months; they began to worry. Her parents tried to call her in Lebanon, but her husband took the phone calls and told them she was ill and could not talk; but that they were not to worry as she had good doctors attending her and would be fine.

"Three more months passed and they still had not heard from her. No-one would take their phone calls; then finally Sylvia's husband called to say she had died suddenly. Her parents felt there was more to this story than an illness. They were poor and could not go to Lebanon themselves; but they got in touch with their local politician. This man was a very caring individual who had known Sylvia as a child. He assured her parents that he would make discreet inquiries.

"After about a month they received the most heartbreaking news. Sylvia's life in Lebanon in this strict Muslim home was bondage; she had been one of four wives and, indeed, her husband did have concubines. Her parents worst predictions had been correct.

"Her parents learned Sylvia had tried to escape from her husband with her two sons. She was caught by her husband's "guards" and returned to him. A few weeks later she had taken one of her husband's cars and tried to escape again. Her husband had anticipated this and set a trap by tampering with the brakes. Sylvia lost control of the car and went over a cliff to her death. The crash decapitated her.

"Sylvia's sons remained in Lebanon; her parents never had a chance to see them and they were told that they would not be able to bring her husband to justice; he was only subject to Islamic law and under the law he had done nothing "rong."

Islam gives men
absolute control of their women

The *Prodigy News Service* reported on the exclusion of women from the Million Man March, saying, "Farrakhan invited black men only – asking women to stay at home and care for their families on the 'holy day,' an exclusionary step that brought an outburst of criticism last week from one-time radical leader Angela Davis." The report said, "Farrakhan has infuriated, feminists and others."[2] They would be more infuriated if they knew Farrakhan once canceled a speaking engagement because a university refused to exclude women from the event. This is not just the quirk of some weird individual. It is consistent with the teachings of the *Quran*, which Farrakhan preaches. This book emphatically teaches women are inferior beings who are to be in subjection to men.

The *Quran* not only gives men the right to have sex with many women, it, also, allows them to have absolute control over their women.

The *Quran* makes it very clear that men are to be in charge of women because men are superior to women. The *Quran* says:""Men are in charge of women, because Allah hath made the one of them to excel the other, and because they spend of their property (for the support of women). So good women are the obedient" (*Quran* 4:34, Pickthal translation).

Islamic scholars say women should obey men because Allah has bestowed more intelligence upon men: "Men have been given authority over women to discipline and control them by the merits of knowledge, intelligence and custody, etc., which God bestowed on some over others."[3]

When it comes to the family inheritance, a woman gets only one-half of a man's share. The *Quran* specifies: "Of the inheritance: if there are Brothers and sisters, The male having twice the share of the female, Thus doth Allah make clear To you, lest ye err" (*Quran* 5:176, Yusufalin translation).

Muslim women are not only subjected to a rough role here, but also hereafter. The *Hadith*, which records additional teachings of Muhammad and like the *Quran* is considered inspired of Allah, says: "The Prophet said, 'I was shown the Hell-fire and that the majority of its dwellers were women'." (*Hadith*, vol. 1, no. 161; vol. 2, no. 161).

The *New York Times* published the story of forty-seven women who attempted to drive their cars in Saudi Arabia and were duly punished: "The crisis in the Gulf last fall spawned a messy and much publicized demonstration by women, who dumped their chauffeurs and drove in convoy, defying an informal ban on driving by women. The incident prompted a vicious campaign against them by religious fanatics."[4]

The government reprisals against the women were mild compared to those of the devout Muslims who branded them "dirty American secularists." One of the women said, "It is like that here in Saudi Arabia, I exist as a person from the belly-button to the knees."

Before Americans get excited about Farrakhan and his religion they need to take a long look at Saudi Arabia where Islamic women are held in sexual slavery by men who see them as a human being only "from the bellybutton to the knees."

Muhammad taught that women have such crooked characters that a man should not even attempt to straighten them out but merely enjoy them. *In Sahih pf al-Bukhari* (part 7, p.80) "Allah's apostle said: The woman is like a rib, if you try to straighten her, she will break ; so if you want to get benefit from her, do so while she still has some crookedness."[5]

The *Quran* specifies that men are to control these "crooked" women by scourgin them.. It commands a man to beat his wife with a scourge if she is unfaithful or guilty of any rebellion: "So good women are the obedient, guarding in secret that which Allah hath guarded. As for those from whom ye fear rebellion, admonish them and banish them to beds apart, and scourge them" (*Quran* 4:34, Pickthal translation).

In some English translations of the *Quran*, Islam seeks to deceive potential converts, by inserting the word "lightly" in parenthesis, so the text reads "scourge (lightly)" or "beat (lightly)." This has no basis in the original Arabic *Quran*, and is apparently a device of modern tricksters. The Arabic word for "scourge" is the same used in reference to beating camels and criminals. Far from lightly tapping his wife, the *Quran* says the husband should use a "scourge."

Scourging is by no means a light spanking. It is done with a whip of multi-strips of leather, sometimes containing pieces of metal and bone to rip open the skin of the one beaten. An Islamic scholar commands men to use the fear of the scourge to keep the wife in line. "Hang up your scourge in a place where your wife can see it."[6]

Women are not only controlled by fear of a beating but also by fear of divorce. This is a very horrible fear in Muslim countries where many women are completely dependent on their husbands for their incomes. The *Quran* outlines the rules by which a man is to divorce his wife and later remarry. These rules are only for the men. They make no provisions for the wife to divorce her husband: "So if a husband divorces his wife (irrevocably), He cannot, after that, re-marry her until after she has married another husband and He has divorced her. In that case there is no blame on either of them if they re-unite, provided they feel that they can keep the limits ordained by God. ... And if he hath divorced her (the third time), then she is not lawful unto him thereafter until she hath wedded another husband. Then if he (the other husband) divorce her it is no sin for both of them that they come together again" (*Quran* 2:230, Yusufali translation).

A revocable divorce is as easy as saying, "I divorce you" twice. For an irrevocable divorce, the man must repeat it three times (*Quran* 2:229, 230).

The writings of al-Bukhari make this clear: "If a man says to his wife, 'Go to your family,' then his intention is to be taken into consideration. Or if someone says to his wife, 'If you become pregnant, then you are divorced thrice;' then, if her pregnancy becomes apparent, she will be regarded as divorced irrevocably! If he wants her back, she must marry and divorce another man first."[7]

While Farrakhan talks about male responsibility, he preaches from a book that allows men to divorce their wives by merely saying "I divorce you." This makes an absolute farce out of the institute of marriage. It also relieves the man of any responsibility; a fact which is highly attractive to young sex obsessed, irresponsible males.

One could wonder why Muhammad, who had such a low opinion of women, surrounded himself with so many wives and concubines? It is hard to imagine any reason other than the pleasure he got from his sex slaves.

Dr. Nawal Sa-dawi, an outstanding Egyptian writer, said, "I want to say that a Christian wife enjoys a secure married life compared to the Muslim woman because she is not afraid of a surprise divorce made by her husband in a day and a night."[8] The Bible does present a woman with a much more secure, exclusive relationship. It says: *For this reason a man shall leave his father and mother and shall be joined to his wife, and the two shall become one flesh. So then, they are no longer two but one flesh. Therefore what God has joined together, let not man put asunder* (Matthew 19:4-6).

"Not Without My Daughter!"

The highest profile American woman who ever suffered Islam's humiliating bondage, is Betty Mahmoody. She married a Muslim man in the US and made the mistake of visiting her husband's home in Iran. Mrs. Mahmoody became his prisoner, unable to leave her house without his permission. She discovered women can be and are kept a virtual prisoner in Islamic countries. Her story was made into the movie, *Not Without My Daughter*, starring Sally Field. Today Mrs. Mahmoody is touring the United States telling women what it is like to be the sex slave of a Muslim.

Mrs. Mahmoody has had to change her name to protect her daughter and herself; she knows that her husband would try to kidnap them and take them back to Iran where she would again become a "prisoner."

Betty Mahmoody lived in a residential area of Detroit, Michigan. She was married to a young Iranian doctor, practicing in the United States; they had a daughter, Mahtob. Her husband became homesick for his family in Iran; and suggested the family take a trip to visit them. Betty was very nervous about this idea; she knew that there was a lot of unrest in that part of the world and did not want to go. However, her husband persuaded her that everything would be fine and so she reluctantly agreed.

Immediately after their arrival, she experienced what it was like to be a woman in a Muslim dominated country. Betty's sister had brought the "chador," the traditional Muslim dress, for her to put on so that she would not get into 'trouble;' this covered her from head to toe including the veil over her face. She was determined however to have a good time for the sake of her husband. She tried to get to know her husband's family and fit in for the short time she was going to be there. She soon discovered that she was facing a wall of extreme prejudice. To her astonishment her husband informed her one day that they were going to remain in Iran. She argued, but her arguments fell on deaf Islamic ears.

When her father became ill in the United States her husband said he would allow her to return to visit him but she could not take her daughter. She said she could not go "not without my daughter." Betty faced the fact that she was a prisoner in Iran and decided that the only way of escape for her and her daughter was to pretend to become the "good Muslim wife." She wore the chador, made friends with members of the family and went to school to learn the teachings of the *Quran*.

After a while, Betty met an Iranian merchant in the bazaar who said he would help her escape to America. She tried to let her family in America know what was happening to her and gave a letter to another American Muslim wife who said she would get the letter out. Betty found out that the control the Muslim husband has over his wife is enormous; the other woman felt obliged to tell her husband of the letter and he beat her severely. In desperation, Betty knew she had to escape immediately. She pursued her merchant contact, who proved as good as his word. She and her daughter escaped, traveling in cars, on horseback and on foot. Her long and arduous journey through the desert took here to safety in Turkey and finally back to the United States. Today she is devoted to alerting Americans to the sexual slavery Islam inflicts upon women.

Newsweek magazine says, "fake marriages hide practices that differ from slavery only in name," in many Muslim countries. "Filipino maids who escaped their Kuwaiti masters in London during the Gulf War told harrowing tales of beatings and rapes," said *Newsweek*. The article titled "Slavery" names "religion" as a cornerstone of slavery. The slaves are obtained through abduction, arranged marriages and fraudulent labor contracts. "Everywhere slavery is practiced, victims tell of beatings, rape, hunger and torture. ... They don't have the most basic of human rights: the right not to be another's property," reports *Newsweek*.[9]

Defenders of Islam try to say many such Arab practices are not doctrines of the *Quran* but cultural traditions. For instance, Sai'd Al-Ashmawy, a former chief justice of Egypt's Supreme Court, wrote a propaganda piece in *Readers Digest*, saying, "Militants insist that women conceal themselves with the hijab, or Arab veil, when outdoors. In Algeria schoolgirls have even been killed for not wearing head scarves. But nowhere does the *Quran* require women to wear a head-to-foot "Islamic" garment. In the Prophet's day, many women went about with their breasts uncovered. What the *Quran* really states is that women should dress more modestly by pulling a cloth across the chest."[10]

Despite the cultural excuse, the facts speak for themselves. When the Muslim man dictates what she can and cannot do it is not cultural; it is a doctrine of the *Quran*. Arab women must have their husband's permission to go outside the house. In Kuwait, Muslims refuse women the right to vote. Muslim women in Arabia must do whatever their husbands say to do; it is the command of the *Quran*. If this is merely culture, then the *Quran* is merely a book inspired by culture, instead of a book inspired by Allah.

Malcolm X, like his successor Louis Farrakhan, once held a rigid perspective on women during his early years with the Black Muslims. Following his split with the Nation of Islam he made a complete turn about on women. He admitted "that any degree of progress can never be separated from the woman. I am proud of our women and the contribution they have made in the struggle for freedom;... in fact they've made a greater contribution than many of us men."

Malcolm X knew what a powerful appeal male dominance held for men. He also came to realize how wrong it was. He set the Nation of Islam Muslim a good example in leaving this sexist group, even if it did cost him his life.

The Islamic religion
uses sex to entice men to kill

The *Quran* not only entices men to join the Islamic movement with sex, it also motivates men to go to war, to kill and die for sex. Allah offered to give his soldiers the women and property of those they killed, which included the women:

"The Prophet said, "Whoever has killed an enemy and has proof of that, will possess his spoils" (*Hadith*, vol. 4, no. 370). The *Quran* says: "Let those fight in the cause of God Who sell the life of this world for the hereafter. To him who fighteth in the cause of God – whether he is slain or gets victory – Soon shall We give him a reward of great (value)" (*Quran* 4:74).

Again, the *Hadith* records that Muhammad followed this practice, taking the women of those he killed: "Allah's Apostle vanquished them by force and their warriors were killed; their children and women were taken as captives. Safiya was taken by Dihya Al-Kalbi and later she belonged to the Allah's Apostle who married her" (*Hadith*, Vol. 2, no. 68). The founder of Islam was a sex obsessed man who found gratification in taking the wives of the men he killed, or conquered, in his wars.

Islamic scholar Ali Dashti wrote, "All the commentaries agree that verse 57 of *Quran* 4 (on Nesa) (chapter 4 of the *Quran*) was sent down after the Jews criticized Mohammad's appetite for women, alleging that he had nothing to do except to take wives."[11]

Muslim scholar Ibn Housham, in his book *Life of the Apostle*, said Muhammad led the Muslims in a war against the Bani Qareza tribe. The tribe threw down their weapons and surrendered to Muhammad. Muhammad told Saad Ibn Muaaz to kill the hundreds of men and divide the women and money between the two of them as war booty.

A Muslim knows if he fights in a revolution for the cause of Allah and wins, he is entitled to the women of the men he kills. But, what if he is killed? Well Islam takes care of this, promising there is sex after death. If he dies fighting for Allah he is promised he will go to paradise and have a hundred Genes (female wonders who pop out of bottles) to satisfy his sexual desires. In killing or dying he stands to win new sexual thrills. Islam promises a great host of virgins to the man who dies fighting for Allah.

Farrakhan talks about family values in his public appearances, but the truth is, Louis Farrakhan, every Mosque in America, and every Muslim teacher in America uses the *Quran*. And the *Quran* advocates wife abuse, strips away the rights of a woman, and undermines American families.

Muslims should either renounce the *Quran* and stop teaching it, or they should publicly admit they have no regard for women's rights and are just using women to gratify their lusts and forward their revolution.

Chapter 7
White men in the valley of death

"It was a wonder this didn't kill them all" a TV news reporter said to me as we looked at the bomb-damaged New York Trade Tower which had just been shaken by a terrorist bomb. Fifty thousand people were in the building the Friday afternoon the bomb rocked the building and jarred our nation. The Muslim terrorism we had read about in the Middle East had come to our shores.

I went to the Brooklyn Mosque where the bombing was planned. It is just across Hudson Bay from the Trade Towers. Between the two buildings stood the Statue of Liberty, the symbol of a freedom that was now facing a new threat from Muslim terrorist within our country.

Muslim terrorist are not "extremist"
they are simply people who believe Islam's teachings
The Muslims who set off the New York bomb were quickly labeled "fanatics" and "extremists." Actually, they were simply dedicated Muslims doing what their *Quran* commands – killing those who deserve to die.

It is very difficult for Americans to face the fact that there is a major world religion that teaches its members to murder. As difficult as it is, there is clear evidence in the teachings of all Muslims that documents this truth.

Muslims teach American white men should be killed

for two reasons: supression of Islam and supression of blacks. Arab Muslims believe they are under divine orders to kill white Americans for political oppression of Islam. America supported Israel in her wars with Islamic nations, helped an Egyptian regime that had signed a peace accord with Israel, attacked the Islamic nation of Iraq, and boycotted the Muslims in Bosnia who sought arms to defend themselves. Furthermore, America is seen as guilty of corrupting morals in the Muslim world through pornography, liquor, sex and drugs. For this the *Quran* demands Americans die.

The Black Muslims believe they are under divine orders to kill white Americans for racial oppression of blacks. Their *Quran* demands the oppressors of human rights must be killed and they are certain their rights have been oppressed by white Americans. In accord with his scriptures, Farrakhan prophesied, "the white man goes down into the valley of death."[1]

Louis Farrakhan arrived at his dangerous beliefs when he left the Christianity he was raised in to embrace Islam. Christianity commands men to forgive their enemies, love their enemies, and "do violence to no man." Islam, in contrast, teaches men should kill their enemies and gives moral and spiritual justification for doing so. Both Christianity and Islam demand justice. Christianity says we must wait upon God to minister justice at the last judgment. Islam says justice must be carried out here and now by its members.

Christianity is the religion of the spiritual man who wishes to love others, live in peace, await justice and be rewarded in heaven. Islam is the religion of the natural man who wishes to indulge in hatred, violence, murder, war, execute his justice now and be rewarded on earth.

This difference is obvious and admitted by Muslim

leaders. "A perfect religion, unlike Christianity, recognizes the necessity of warfare," said the Iranian Muslim teacher Ayatollah Sayyid Mahmuc Taleqani. Islam, understandably, is the religion of choice for revolutionaries, terrorists, and people who wish to start a class or racial war. It is a religion that was tailor made for Louis Farrakhan. The *Quran* gives him the moral and spiritual justification he needs to retaliate against white people.

Peace-loving Muslims try to escape the *Quran's* commands to kill by quoting this passage from the *Quran*: "Fight in the way of Allah against those who fight against you, but begin not hostilities. Lo! Allah loveth not aggressors" (*Quran* 2:190, Pickthal tranlation).

The catch word in the passage is "aggressors." Those who criticize Islam, get in the way of Islam, or try to leave the Islamic faith, are classified "aggressors," who deserves to die.

The defenders of Islam love to point out that history is full of fighting and killing by Christians. There is one big difference. When a Christian kills he is disobeying the teachings of his Bible. But when a Muslim kills he is obeying the teachings of his *Quran*.

Most Muslims are congenial, nice, peace-loving people. They would never think of killing anyone and they despise the terrorists who do. But, every Mosque in the world teaches the *Quran* and the *Hadith*. And every Muslim in the world professes to believe these books represent the will of Allah.

Not every Christian will end up loving his enemies and turning the other cheek to his assailants, but those that do must credit their Christian teachings. Not every Muslim will end up being a killer, but those that do must credit their Islamic teachings.

Islam teaches ten reasons every Muslim should be a murderer. They are laborsome to study, but they enable you to understand why so many Muslims are killers and terrorist and why Islam is such a deadly threat.

1. Muslims should kill to bring justice to those who infringe on human rights

The *Quran* says it is necessary to fight and kill to prevent evil men from destroying human rights and corrupting the earth. The *Quran* says, "If Allah had not repelled some men by others the earth would have been corrupted" (*Quran* 2:251, Pickthal translation). Ayatollah Murtada Mutahhari taught this passage clearly demanded fighting those who suppressed human rights: "No one should have any doubts that the most sacred form of jihad (an Islamic holy war) and war is that which is fought in defense of humanity and of human rights."[2]

Does Allah want black Americans to actually go to war against white people? It is very easy to build a case for it from the teachings of Islam. Mehdi Abedi and Gary Legenhausen, in the introduction to their book, *Jihad and Shahadat* (jihad means a holy war, Shahadat means martyrdom, or dying in a holy war), wrote, "What then, constitutes a just cause for the initiation of jihad'? There is no one answer upon which all Muslims are in agreement. We may, however, list the most widely accepted reasons for going to war:

1. Defense
2. Revolution against tyranny
3. Establishment of the shari'ah (the Islamic law)

There would be wide-spread agreement with going to war and killing in defense of your country. The second reason is more controversial. It means killing to overcome tyranny could justify a war by American blacks against a white government which blacks perceive to be unfair. And the third reason, to impose Islamic law, would justify fighting against the United States or any government except Iran and Sudan, which already are governed by the teachings of Muhammad.

Islam teaches governments which are judged to be unfair to the people should be attacked: "Here is another phase of jihad ... waging war against the despots, so that no one can reign as a tyrant ... It is the duty of every Muslim to invite the despots onto the straight path."[3]

Islam requires Muslims to help American blacks who feel they are suffering under white oppressors even if they do not ask for help: "The requesting of help is yet another issue. It is permissible or moreover obligatory for us to render aid to the oppressed regardless of whether they apply to us for help. The simple fact that the oppressed are oppressed, that an oppressive regime has erected a barrier for its own well-being, preventing a nation from becoming aware of the call wherein lies the prosperity and happiness of that nation, which call they are sure to accept if they hear and become aware of it, prompts Islam to say that we can break that barrier."[4]

Salim Muwakkil warns that America's racial conditions put her on the road to a solemn day of national reckoning: "If the politics of polarization continue unabated, the country will suffer irreparable damage. Not only are working-class whites rejecting civil rights goals, but African-American youth increasingly are rejecting the idea of racial reconciliation. ... U. S. leaders seem content to seek no-fault solutions that merely postpone the necessary national reckoning."[5]

Farrakhan is predicting and promoting the destruction

of all white Americans. He says they have abused the rights of black men and are going "down into the valley of death." Farrakhan not only supports this with the *Quran*, but even twists the Bible to prove white people are evil and deserve to be destroyed. Quoting from the fifth chapter of James, Farrakhan said, *Go to now, you rich man, weep and howl, for your miseries that shall come upon you* (James 5:1). This, my beloved Black brothers and sisters, Elijah Muhammad wants you to know, is the end of the white man's power to rule and dominate the lives of Black people the world over. This is the beginning of their sorrows. But, as the white man, in his sorrow, lifts up his eyes and sees the end of his days, as the white man goes down into the valley of death, never to rise again, his anger is so great that his mind is set on the destruction of God's people (the Black Muslims). And so we are warned."[6]

Farrakhan is doing a good job of obeying Al-Anfal, who said, "O Apostle! rouse the believers to the fight." This appears easy to do in the United States' present racial climate. Business executive Ian M. Rolland said, "Islam gave many disenfranchised African-Americans a right that they felt Christianity did not give – the right to fight back against the oppressor ... it allows Muslims to use force to rectify the injustices of others."[7]

If white people are oppressing the blacks, Islam says they must be killed to stop them from corrupting the earth.

2. Muslims should kill to
punish those who do not believe in Islam

The *Quran* commands Muslims to kill all those who refuse to repent and accept the Islamic faith: "But when the forbidden months are past, then fight and slay the Pagans wherever ye find them, and seize them, beleaguer them, and lie in wait for them in every stratagem (of war); but if they repent, and establish regular prayers and practice regular charity, then open the way for them: for God is Oft-forgiving, Most Merciful" (*Quran* 9:5, Yusufali translation).

Dr. Muhammad Said al-Buti, one of the most eminent scholars of the Islamic world wrote, "The verse (9:5 of the *Quran*) does not leave any room in the mind to conjecture about what is called defensive war. This verse asserts that Holy War which is demanded in Islamic law, is not defensive war (as the Western students of Islam would like to tell us) because it could legitimately be an offensive war. That is the apex and most honorable of all Holy wars."[8]

When Muhammad started his religion he said, "There is no compulsion in religion," (*Quran* 2:5, Pickthal translation) and told his followers not to fight anyone. Later, after he gained power, he started ordering his followers to kill, struggle and fight against non-believers with the sword to spread their religion. Today Muslims follow his example, talking tolerance until they are in power and then beginning to fight against non-believers.

While American Muslims are declaring, "there is no compulsion in the faith - No one is forced to be a Muslim" The *Quran* gives only two alternatives to joining their religion: to die or pay a heavy tax imposed on unbelievers. The *Hadith* says, "Our Prophet, the Messenger of our Lord, has ordered us to fight you till you worship Allah alone or give Jizya (the heavy tax forced on unbelievers)" (*Hadith*, Vol. 4, no. 386).

The Islamic scholar Ibn Hisham documents that Muhammad killed those who would not accept his religion: "Muhammad sent Khalid Ibn al-Walid to the tribe of the children of Haritha and told him: 'Call them to accept Islam before you fight with them. If they respond, accept that from them, but if they refuse, fight them.' Khalid told them: 'Accept Islam and spare your life.' They entered Islam by force. He brought them to Muhammad. Muhammad said to them: 'Had you not accepted Islam I would have cast your heads under your feet'."[9]

The *Quran* only guarantees the right to life to those who believe in Allah. "Never should a believer kill a believer" (*Quran* 4.92).

Ibn Kathir says that Muhammad's followers met a man and asked him to become a Muslim. He asked them, "What is Islam?" They explained that to him. He said, "What if I refuse it? What would you do to me?" They answered, "We would kill you." Despite that, he refused to become a Muslim and they killed the poor man after he went and bade his wife farewell. She continued to weep over his corpse for days until she died of grief over her slain beloved who was killed for no reason.[10]

The great Islamic professors and the judges of Islamic legal court documented their position that those who would not convert to their religion should be killed. In a favorite book of Muslims, *The Spirit of Islamic Religion*, which they have reprinted nine times, it says: "Islam has approved war so that the Word of God becomes supreme. This is war for the cause of God (Holy War). Muhammad, therefore, sent his ambassadors to eight kings and princes in the neighborhood of the Arab Peninsula to call them to embrace Islam. They rejected his call. Thus, it became incumbent on the Muslims to fight them. ... Islamic law demands that before Muslims start fighting infidels (unbelievers), they first deliver the message of Islam to them. It was proven that the prophet never fought people before he called them to embrace Islam first. He used to command his generals to do so also."[11]

The respected Muslim teacher, Ibn Hisham, says, "Muhammad sent Khalid Ibn al-Walid to the tribe of the children of Haritha and told him: 'Call them to accept Islam before you fight with them. If they respond, accept that from them, but if they refuse, fight them.' Khalid told them: 'Accept Islam and spare your life.' They entered Islam by force. He brought them to Muhammad. Muhammad said to them: 'Had you not accepted Islam I would have cast your heads under your feet'."[12]

On November 13, 1995, Muslims bombed a U.S.-run military training facility in Riyadh, Saudi Arabia injuring 60 and killing five Americans and one Indian. The Islamic Movement for Change, credited with the attack, had been sending faxed warnings throughout the year of what would happen if the thousands of Americans and British did not leave Saudi Arabia. On the fateful day, they placed a 150 to 225-pound bomb outside the building where Americans were working. They were faithfully carrying out the command of the *Quran* to kill those who do not believe in Allah.[13]

3. Muslims should kill Christians and Jews for disobeying their scriptures

The *Quran* specifically says Jews and Christians should be killed for disobeying their scriptures: "Fight those who believe not in God nor the Last Day, nor hold that forbidden which hath been forbidden by God and His Apostle, nor acknowledge the religion of Truth, (even if they are) of the People of the Book (Jews and Christians), until they pay the Jizya with willing submission, and feel themselves subdued" (*Quran* 9:29, Yusufali translation). The

Christian and Jew have one alternative to death; submit to Islam.

Farrakhan threatened Jews during the Savior's Day· speech in 1984. He told the Jews who were heckling Jesse Jackson, "If you harm this brother, it'll be the last one you ever harm."[14] Farrakhan was being true to the *Quran*.

Farrakhan continues such assaults against Jews, telling his people the Jews keep blacks down. This strategy appears to be working. A *New York Times* poll taken in 1994 showed 40 percent of blacks agree that most Jews are against progress by blacks.

During the British occupation of Egypt, Hasan Al-Banna called for jihad against the British. He appealed to reports of sayings of Muhammad *(Hadith)*, the *Quran* and to medieval legalists, to prove that jihad is justified against all non-Muslims, Christians as well as pagans, whether they fight against the Muslims or not.[15]

Today, loyal Muslims carried out Allah's orders by killing dozens of Christian pastors in the Sudan after Islamic law was imposed in that country.[16]

The Washington Times reported, "In the Sudan you can buy a human being for as little as $15. Marauding Muslims, armed by the Sudanese government, tare through small southern Sudanese villages, kill the men, destroy property and ride off with women and children in tow; they are marched north and sold into slavery as workers, sex partners and breeders." The villages are comprised largely of black Christians. One young victim told an investigator for Anti-Slavery International that "he had been enslaved by an Arab master where he saw that other male slaves had had their achilles tendons cut when they refused to convert to Islam. Under threat of the same fate, the boy 'converted" and later escaped," according to the *Times*.[17]

In southern Egypt the *Quran*'s command to kill Christians is being faithfully carried out today. The Associated Press reportes that fear has gripped the Christian village of Azbit el-Iqbat following Muslim's repeated murders of their Christian neighbors. On February 24, 1996 three Muslims stormed the town and in a 15-minute outburst of violence, gunned down eight people. At 7:15 p.m., the three clean-shaven young men went running into the village. They broke down the door on Aziz Boutros Suleiman's house. As the children screamed and his wife ran for cover they shot the 50-year-old father of 10 to death. Then they ran to St. George's Church and shot down 6 more only several feet from the church. The church displays a picture of St. George slaying the dragon, an ironic contradiction to what was happening outside. "We don't sleep at night," said the cousin of one of the victims. "How are we going to work if we're too scared to sleep? How are we going to make money?"

In the two years since the town of 5,000 was pronounced "secured," 28 people have been killed. AP said, "Human rights groups say the assailants increasingly kill civilians, often minority Cioptic Christians, in a campaign to replace Egypt's government with strict Islamic rule – and to instill fear among those who disagree."[18]

Islam offers two justifications for killing Christians and Jews. First, for trying to lead Muslims astray. The *Quran* says, "It is the wish of a section of the People of the Book to lead you astray" (*Quran* 3:69, Yusufali translation). On November 13, 1995, Islamic militants bombed a U.S. run military training facility in Riyadh, Saudi Arabia injuring 60 and killing five Americans and one Indian. The Islamic Movement for Change, credited with the attack, had been sending faxed warnings throughout the year telling what would happen if the thousands of American and British did not leave Saudi Arabia. When they stayed, they were murdered. The Christian British were outrageously offensive to Islam because they disobeyed the laws of Allah and were a bad influence on Muslims.[19]

The second justification for killing Christians and Jews is they have not obeyed the teachings of the scriptures. The *Quran* says they are condemned because "they worship their rabbis and their monks, and the Messiah the son of Mary, as gods besides Allah; they were ordered to serve one God only. There is no god but Him" (*Quran* 9:31).

Muslim scholars justify Muhammad's slaughter of the Jews, as well as their modern day attacks on them, by saying they violated the teachings of Judaism and conspired against Islam.

An Arab friend of mine, who cannot reveal his identity without risking his life, wrote in his book *Behind the Veil*: "The time will come when East and West, as well as politicians and military personnel all over the world will realize that the real military danger is the Islamic community. When the needed military power becomes available to them, they will wage wars and invade other countries!" He gave up a medical practice and came to America to tell us how Muslims slaughtered Christians in Egypt and what they plan to do in the United States.

4. Muslims should kill
to follow Muhammad's example

Islam says Muslims should kill in order to follow the example of Muhammad, the messenger of Allah: "Verily in the messenger of Allah ye have a good example" (*Quran*

33.21, Pickthal). The Hadith says their "good example" killed many people: "When Muhammad was told that Ibn Khatal was taking refuge in the Kabah, he ordered, "Kill him." He was butchered (*Hadith*, vol. 3, no. 72).

Muhammad had one man killed for making a joke. This poor fellow noticed how the Muslims had dirt on their foreheads from bowing to the ground in prayer. So, to make a joke, he rubbed a hand-full on his forehead and said, "This is sufficient for me." The Muslims murdered him in cold blood for his joke (*Hadith*, vol. 2, no. 173).

History documents the fact that Muhammad led 27 invasions of neighboring countries, personally fighting in nine of these and killed thousands. In addition, he ordered his followers to conduct at least 47 other invasions that reigned death on neighboring countries.

Muhammad's successor, Abu Bakr Al-Sedeik, followed the example of this "prophet of God" after his death. He said, "know you that the Apostle of God intended to invade Syria, however God had taken him, and by God, I am intending to lead the Muslim heroes to Al-Sham ... That Apostle of God has told me before his death: 'I have been granted the Eastern and Western Spheres and what is granted to me is an order."[20] He followed Muhammad's example and carried on the Islamic slaughter Muhammad had begun.

5. Muslims must kill
to stop criticism of the *Quran*

Salman Rushdie has forced the world to face the frightening fact that Islam does require killing. Rushdie, a member of the Islamic faith, wrote a novel called the *Satanic Verses* which brought a cry of blasphemy from many Muslims. Muslims found references to the *Quran* that were offensive. The furor over the book quickly grew into an international issue. Demonstrators protested the book in the streets of Teheran and called for the death of the author. The outcry grew across the Islamic world, demanding the death of Rushdie and for retaliations against the book publishers and the bookstores in Britain and the United States that were selling it. A demonstration at the American Center in Islamabad, Pakistan, on February 12, 1989, resulted in riots and the death of five Pakistanis.

An Islamic court sentenced Rushdie to death. They have even put a one million dollar bounty on his head. It is reported to be costing the British government one million dollars a year to provide Rushdie with security.

Islam does not allow freedom of speech. The *Quran* denounces those that "speak a lie concerning Allah knowingly" (*Quran* 3:75, Pickthal translation). Anyone who criticizes the faith must be killed.

The 100-year-old Jewish poet Abu Efek wrote poems critical of Muhammad and Muhammad ordered him killed. Ibn Housham, in volume three of his *The Life of the Apostle*, said Muhammad ordered: "Bring me this cynic, so Salem Ibn Omeir was sent to kill him while he was lying at the yard of his house – he killed him by piercing his sword against Abu Efek's liver."

It is reported that thirty-seven journalist have been killed for writing things Muslims perceive to be critical about their faith.

One exiled feminist author cannot go home without being killed because she offended Muslims. Taslima Nasrin, of Bangladesh, is forced to live in Helsinki, Finland since an Indian newspaper quoted her as calling for changes in the *Quran*, the Muslim holy book. Taslima denies this, but said she did call for changes in Islamic laws that restrict women. Muslim extremists offered $5,000 to the person who kills Taslima. A Bangladeshi court has charged her with blasphemy and is going to try her in absentia.

6. Muslims should kill to expand the kingdom of Islam

The *Quran* orders Muslims to kill in order to persuade those who remain to join Islam: "Make war on them until idolatry is no more and Allah's religion reigns supreme" (*Quran* 8:39, Dawood translation).

An Islamic scholar said, "When the prophet migrated from Mecca to Medina, God ordered him to fight those who fought him only. Then when the chapter of Repentance was revealed, God commanded His prophet to fight anyone who did not become a Muslim from among the Arabs, whether (that person) fought him or not."[21]

The most famous book about Muhammad's life says: "When Muhammad conquered Mecca and the Arabs realized that they were not able to wage war against Muhammad, they accepted the Islamic faith. But some of the infidels continued to be as they were. Then suddenly Muhammad sent someone to announce to the Tribe of Quraysh (he) was going to give the infidels a respite for four months, and after that there would not be a covenant except the covenant of the sword and war ... anyone who did not become a Muslim fled the Arabian Peninsula.[22] Ibn Hisham also quoted Muhammad's threatening words: "No two religions are to exist in the Arab Peninsula."[23]

Muhammad made it very plain that people must choose between accepting him as the Prophet and Allah as their God, or dying. "I have been ordered by God to fight with people till they bear testimony to the fact that there is no God but Allah and that Mohammed is his messenger, and that they establish prayer and pay Zakat (the Islamic tax), said Muhammad. "If they do it, their blood and their property are safe from me...."[24]

A respected Islamic scholar, Dr. Buti, is a rare Muslim. He tells the truth, saying Muslims should use force to make people embrace Islam whether they mean it or not: "It may be said, 'What is the value of a faith in Islam which is a result of a threat? Abu Sufyan, one moment ago, was not a believer, then he believed after he was threatened by death.' We say to those who question: 'What is required of an infidel or the one who confuses other gods with God, is to have his tongue surrender to the religion of God and to subdue himself to the prophethood of Muhammad. But his heartfelt faith is not required at the beginning. It will come later'."[25]

This honest, Islamic scholar makes it clear that Muslims are to engage in offensive wars, "The Holy War, as it is known in Islamic Jurisprudence, is basically an offensive war. This is the duty of Muslims in every age when the needed military power becomes available to them. This is the phase in which the meaning of Holy War has taken its final form. Thus the apostle of God said: 'I was commanded to fight the people until they believe in God and his message'."[26]

World rule is the declared goal of Islam, "Islam is a revolutionary ideology and program which seeks to alter the social order of the whole world and rebuild it in conformity with its own tenets and ideals," writes S. Abul a'la). "'Muslim' is the title of that International Revolutionay Party organized by Islam to carry into effect its revolutionary program. And 'Jihad' refers to that revolutionary struggle and utmost exertion which the Islamic Party brings into play to achieve this objective."[27]

At Farrakhan's 1991 Saviors Day celebration in Chicago's Christ Universal Temple, a Nation of Islam leader told the audience they: "Must lay a faith for a new government, we must lay a faith for a new world order. ... Our father which art in heaven, hallowed be thy name, thy kingdom come.... not in the sky in the sweet by and by, after we die, but something sound on the ground while we are still around...we must be about the serious work of laying the faith of government divine government, god's government, here on the earth, we must have some of this good earth we can call our own."

Ruh Allah Khumayni, the Muslim scholar and author says, "[By] means of jihad and enjoining the good and forbidding the evil, [the jurists] must expose and overthrow tyrannical rulers and rouse the people so that the universal movement of all alert Muslims can establish Islamic government in place of tyrannical regimes?"[28]

Islamics have made it very clear by their writings and their actions that they have no regard for human rights. They are convinced Allah wants them to kill those who resist the spread of Islam. History demonstrates that when they gain the power, they carry out Allah's orders to kill.

7. Muslims should kill
to stop people from leaving Islam

The *Quran* provides no mercy for those who forsake the Islamic faith. It says, "if they turn back (to enmity) then take them and kill them wherever ye find them, and choose no friend nor helper from among them" (*Quran* 4.89). Many Muslim commentators agree that this verse in the *Quran* refers to those who have renounced Islam. Islamic scholar Al-

Bukhari documents that Muhammad said, "The one who changes his religion should be killed."

Muhammad said: "If they desert you, seize them and put them to death wherever you find them" (*Quran* 4:89, Dawood translation). The *Hadith* repeats, "The Prophet said, if somebody (a Muslim) discard his religion, kill him" (*Hadith*, vol. 4, no. 260).

The *Hadith* claims that no one ever leaves Islam: "He then asked, 'Does anybody amongst those who embrace his religion become displeased and renounce the religion afterwards?' I (Muhammad) replied, 'NO'" (*Hadith*, vol. 1, nos. 6 and 48).

Throughout history Islam fought the Apostasy Wars against people who tried to leave the faith. Al-Saiouty said, "When the Arabs became apostates, Abu-Bakr and his followers attacked them and fought against them until they brought them back to Islam."

In Islam there is no such thing as freedom of religion, or freedom of choice. No Muslim is free to quit the faith, or convert to another faith. The penalty for doing so is death.

On August 6, 1977, the Egyptian newspaper *al-Ahram* said, "The state assembly has approved a bill to enact the penalty for apostasy. The apostate who intentionally relinquishes Islam by explicit declaration or decisive deed must be put to death. Apostasy is established by one confirmation or by the testimony of two men. The apostate is forbidden to administer his properties. He will be given 30 days to repent before the execution of the sentence of death. But if the one converted to Christianity was 10-14 years old, he will only be scourged fifty times."

Brutalizing those who leave the faith is already being practiced in the United States. The *Saturday Evening Post* did an article entitled, "The Black Muslims Are a Fraud" in February, 1965. In it Aburey Barnette told what happens to Muslims who try to leave Islam. She wrote, "A great deal could be written about the violent physical attacks some blacks have suffered after leaving the Nation of Islam."

On February 21, 1965 Malcolm X was killed for changing his religion. He had just finished giving a public lecture at the Audubon Ballroom in New York City, when three black men shot him to death. Malcolm X had become the chief spokesman for the Nation of Islam. He recruited thousands of converts, more than anyone in the history of the organization. But he became dissatisfied after learning of Elijah's extra-marital affairs. He decided to leave the Nation of Islam. Seven months later he was assassinated by three Muslims. Betty Shabazz, the widow of Malcolm X was quoted in *Time* magazine, stating she believed Farrakhan had a role in her husband's assassination in 1991.[29] Malcolm X's crime was leaving the Nation of Islam. For this he had to die.

8. Muslims should kill
to stop their opposition

The *Quran* teaches Muslims have a duty to kill people who oppose Islam: "Slay them. Such is the reward of those who suppress faith" (*Quran* 2.19, Yusufali translation). That death can be tortuous and barbaric: "The punishment of those who wage war against God and His Apostle, and strive with might and main for mischief through the land is: execution, or crucifixion, or the cutting off of hands and feet from opposite sides, or exile from the land: that is their disgrace in this world, and a heavy punishment is theirs in the Hereafter" (*Quran* 5:33, Yusufali translation).

There is a cafeteria of choices for the Muslims. They

can exile them from the land, or they can cutoff hands and feet; or they can execute them by crucifixion! In addition, Allah will punish them heavily in the "Hereafter."

This Islamic teaching has been obeyed throughout history. Ali Dashti details the Islamic use of barbaric punishments like cutting off hands, feet, ears, tongues and gouging out eye. This is done without due process of law.[30]

Farrakhan appears to take this teaching very literally. He warns that any informer's "mouth" can become the instrument of "his doom." This includes any black policeman who would inform on a black man. He made this thinly veiled threat to any informer: "That's an enemy to his people. Now, the white man has found that he has outlived his usefulness, so he's making him (the informer) known to all of us. Now see, he can't go among whites and you know he can't come among us! Is that right? Should we love an informer? No. Any Black Man, I don't care what police department you work for, you should REFUSE to take a job that makes you spy on your Black Brother for your enemy! You must remember, "Stool Pigeon," that white people do not need you to spy on us. They have enough electronic equipment to do that job for them. So Black brother, Black sister, be careful how you use your mouth, because your mouth can become the instrument of your own doom."[31]

When Joe Walker, New York Editor of *Muhammad Speaks* interviewed Farrakhan he asked him about the murder of seven people in which the *New York Times* implicated The Nation of Islam. Farrakhan responded by blaming the murders on "The Hypocrite and the agents (of their enemies) in the ranks of the Muslims."[32]

The problem with his answer is that the killers were doing exactly what Muhammad did and what he taught his followers to do. It is what obedient Muslims have done throughout history – kill those who oppose Islam.

9. Muslims should kill to obtain earthly rewards

Killing brings temporal rewards here and now in the world of Islam. The killer is rewarded with the spoils of his victim: "The Prophet said, 'Whoever has killed an enemy and has proof of that, will possess his spoils'" (*Hadith*, vol. 4, no. 370).

Killing for Allah brings the best of rewards, because it is the best of deeds: "Allah's apostle was asked, 'What is the best deed?" he replied, 'To believe in Allah and his Apostle.' The questioner then asked, 'What is the next?' he replied, 'To participate in jihad (religious fighting) in Allah's cause" (*Hadith*, vol. 1, no. 25).

To make it into the Allah's elite, you must participate in religious fighting. This demonstrates the sincerity of your faith and your love for Allah. The second best thing you could ever do in your lifetime is 'To participate in jihad in Allah's cause'."

Farrakhan dangles the promise of ruling the land after the white man is out of the way before his followers.

10. Muslims should kill to gain rewards in heaven

Muslims are assured that if they die while killing for Allah it guarantees they will go to heavenly rewards: "Think not of those who were slain in the way of God as dead. Nay, they are alive, finding their sustenance with their Lord" (*Quran* 3:169, Yusufali translation)

Only will those who die killing for Allah will be rewarded with the highest status in heaven. Islam says their fighting puts them in the circle of the most virtuous: "The

Prophet said, 'Above every virtue there is another virtue, but there is no virtue higher than being killed in the way of God'."[33]

Participating in a holy war brings the promise of great honor. "In the book, *Safinat al-Bihar,* there is a story of a man named Khaythumah (or Khathimah) who sought the great honor of dying while fighting for Allah: "At the time of the battle of Badr, he and his son were both keen to take part in the fighting and to get killed. They argued with each other. In the end they drew lots. The son won, and accordingly went to the battlefield where he laid down his life. Some time later, the father had a dream in which he saw his son living a very happy life, who told him that God's promise had come true.

"The old father came to the Prophet and narrated the dream. He told the Prophet that though he was too old and too weak to fight, he was desirous of taking part in the fighting and falling a *shahid* (a matyr for Allah). He requested the Prophet to pray to God to grant him his desire. The Prophet prayed accordingly. Within less than a year the old man not only had the good fortune of taking part in the battle of Uhud, but also of achieving *shahadat.*"[34]

Mutahhari explained the aspects of dying as a martyr for Islam: "Shahadat has two basic elements: (a) the life is sacrificed for a cause; and (b) the sacrifice is made consciously. Usually in the case of *shahadat,* an element of crime is involved. As far as the victim is concerned, the death is sacred; but the action of the killers is a heinous crime. *Shahadat* is heroic and admirable, because it results from a voluntary, conscious and selfless action. It is the only type of death which is higher, greater and holier than life itself.[35]

"Jihad is a door to paradise, but it is not open to all and sundry," says Mutahhari. "Not everyone is worthy of it; not everyone is elected to become a muj~hid. God has opened this door for his chosen friends only. A position of *muj~hid* is so high that we cannot call him simply God's friend. He is God's chosen friend."[36]

The dedicated Muslims are willing to die in fighting for Allah, assured they will go to heaven, be greatly honored and lay on couches of silk, surrounded by all matter of fruits and virgin girls.

These Islamic orders to kill are being taught to millions of Muslims in Mosques throughout America. Farrakhan hides Islam's murderous intentions in order to plans to survive. He warned his followers, "Samson ... pushed the temple down, but he killed himself as he did so. Any fool can die, but it takes a wise man to live! A true revolutionary is not a man who seeks to die, he's a man who seeks to live and out maneuver his enemy. ... I think that the worse thing that a Black Man could say ... is, 'I am a revolutionary ... in warfare you must learn the art of camouflage'."[37]

But some times the camouflage is forgotten and true intentions slip out, as when a Lieutenant in Farrakhan's army shouted, "I do not want to know how many of you are willing to die for Allah, I want to know how many of you are willing to KILL FOR ALLAH?"

The Religion That is Raping America

Chapter 8
Ministry of lies

Not since the Germans told the Jews they were going into the gas chambers to take a shower have so many people been deceived by such dangerous lies as Farrakhan and Islam are telling. This religion is a fantasy created by deceivers with a passion for power, sex, land and money. Behind a mask of piety it seduces its followers to give up their lives and their souls to pursue their leader's dark goals. It was born in a bloody revolution and it has been spread by endless, merciless wars. Even worse, it has been spread by lies that lead people away from the true God.

David Koresh and Jim Jones were religious deceivers who led a few hundred followers to death. But, compared to the Muslim leaders, they were saints. The followers of Muhammad have deceived hundreds of millions of people and stained the planet with blood. Islam remains the most wide-spread deception the religious world has ever witnessed.

To the devout, and sincere followers of this faith its name, *Islam*, means "surrender" to Allah. And masses of well meaning people who meant to surrender to the true God of heaven, ended up under the control of power hungry deceivers like Muhammad, Khomeni, and now Farrakhan.

There is a battle raging in today's world between Islam and Christianity for the souls of men. Islam's most formidable weapon in this battle is an arsenal of misinformation. They will tell any imaginable lie to entice people away from Christianity and into their fold. Islam is a ministry of lies. Those who embrace these lies live without a true guide and go into eternity without a true hope.

Lie No. 1: Islam has an errorless
revelation from Almighty God

Muslims stand up with a straight face and declare they have an error-free revelation from Almighty God. But if you take the time to look at what their "revelation" says, you see it is full of ridiculous teachings such as:

You can cure your diseases by drinking camel urine: "So the Prophet ordered them to go the herd of camels and to drink their milk and urine (as a medicine)" (*Hadith*, vol. 1, no. 234).

Muhammad cut the moon in half with his sword. (*Hadith*, vol. 4, nos. 830,931,832; vol. 5, nos. 208, 209, 210, 211; vol. 5, nos. 387, 389, 390)..

The sun sets each evening in a muddy bog: "when he reached the setting-place of the sun, he found it setting in a muddy spring" (*Quran*, 18:86).

You must face Mecca when relieving yourself (Hadith, vol. 1, nos. 146, 147, 150, 151) and use only your left hand for cleaning yourself (*Hadith*, vol. 1, nos. 155,156).

Satan urinates into the ears of those who go to sleep during prayers (*Hadith*, vol. 2, no. 245).

All dogs must be killed, for they frightened the angels away: "Allah's Apostle ordered that the dogs should be killed" (*Hadith*, vol. 4, no. 539, 540).

You can't pray after eating garlic because Allah will not hear your prayers if you have bad breadth (*Hadith*, vol. 1, no. 628, vol. 9, no. 86).

You can't pray if you have gastridous, for if you commit the sin of "hadath," (passing of gas through the anus) while you are praying, Allah will not hear your prayers

(*Hadith,* vol. 1, no. 628; vol. 9, no. 86).

Muhammad, the Apostle of Allah, declared the souls of martyrs are in the bodies of green birds dwelling in paradise (*Hadith,* vol. 1, p. xxviii).

A Rip Van Winkle story of seven men and their animals who slept for 309 years which is found in Greek and Arabian lore, is the truth (*Quran* 18:9-26).

A "she" camel became a prophet (*Quran* 7:73-77,85; 91:14; 54:29).

Allowing urine on your body or clothes can send you to hell. Once the Prophet, while passing one of the graveyards of Medina or Mecca, heard the voices of two persons being tortured in their graves. The Prophet then added, "yes! [they are being tortured for a major sin]. Indeed, one of then never saved himself from being soiled with his urine." (*Hadith,* vol. 1, chap. 57, no. 215)

Jinnis, those fairy-like creatures which are released from Aladdin's lamp in *The Arabian Nights,* have found their way into the Islamic religion. Allah is said to have created the Jinnis from smokeless fire (*Quran,* 55:16). Once some "Jinns" came to hear the *Quran* preached, were converted and went out as Islamic preachers: "Behold, We turned towards thee a company of Jinns (quietly) listening to the Qur'an: when they stood in the presence thereof, they said, "Listen in silence!" When the (reading) was finished, they returned to their people, to warn (them of their sins)" (*Quran* 46.29).

Louis Farrakhan ought to start drinking urine, killing dogs, calling genies out of bottle and chasing the sun into its muddy bog. Or, he ought to stand up and admit that he does not really believe Islam has a revelation from God.

In addition to such absurdities, the Islamic revelation is riddled with historical errors, such as:

Nimrod threw Abraham into a fire (*Quran* 21:68,69 and 9:69) when Nimrod actually died hundreds of years before Abraham was born.

Moses was adopted by Pharoah's wife (*Quran* 28:8,9) when in reality it was Pharoah's daughter (Exodus 2:5).

The flood took place in Moses' day (*Quran* 7:136, 7:59) – actually in Noah's time.

The virgin Mary was the sister of Aaron, when Aaron lived two thousands years before: "At length she brought The (babe) to her people, Carrying him (in her arms), They said: 'O Mary! Truly a strange thing Has thou brought! O sister of Aaron!" (*Quran* 19:27, 28).

Birds dropped stones of baked clay on the elephant riding armies of Abrah as they attacked Mecca (*Quran*, 105:1-5). The historical record says they withdrew when a smallpox epidemic broke out among the troops.[1]

Haman lived in Egypt during the time of Moses and built the tower of Babel for Pharoah (*Quran* 28:38), when he actually lived in Persia and was in the service of King Ahasuerus, according to both secular history and the book of Esther in the Bible.

Besides the absurdities and the inaccuracies of the Islamic revelation, their most holy books, the *Quran,* contradicts itself on numerous points. These contradictions provide conclusive proof the *Quran* is not the infallible word of God.

The *Quran* gives two differing stories on how long creation took. First, it says the Lord "created the earth in two days ... in four days provided it with sustenance ... In two days He formed the sky into seven heavens," for a total of 8 days. (*Quran* 41:9,10,12) Later, it says, "Your Lord is God, who in six days created the heavens and the earth and then ascended the throne."(*Quran* 10:3)

Islam contradicts itself on how Muhammad received the *Quran*. First, the *Quran* said, "Gabriel ... revealed to you the Koran" (*Quran* 2:97); later it says "The Holy Spirit brought it down from your Lord" (*Quran* 16:102).

The *Quran* even contradicts itself within one single chapter. The fourth chapter says a man can have four wives if he treats they justly, "But if ye fear that you shall not treat them fairly, then only one." (*Quran* 4:3) Later in the chapter it turns around and says, "You will not be able to deal equally between your wives however much you wish to do so." (*Quran* 4:129)

The *Quran* cannot decide whether the Bible is true or not. First it tells people to believe in the previous scripture (*Quran* 2:136; 4:136). It urges all to "observe the Torah (the Jewish writings) and the Gospel and that which is revealed to you from your Lord" (*Quran* 5:68). The *Quran* says when you are in doubt about Muhammad's teachings you should "ask those who read the Book before thee" (*Quran* 10:94). So, Islam declares faith in: Moses' Torah, David's Psalms and Jesus' gospels.

Then the *Quran* turns around and declares these same scriptures are unreliable because those who "used to hear the word of Allah, then altered it after they had understood it, and they know (this)," and of those who are "illiterate: they know not the Book but only (from) hearsay, and they do but conjecture. Woe! Then to those who write the Book with their hands they say, This is from Allah; so that they may take for it a small price" (*Quran* 2:75, 78-79 Ali translation). So, they say, this leaves only the *Quran* as a dependable word from God. This so-called corruption of the Bible is known as *tahrif,* or alteration.

When Islam tries to say the original scriptures have been altered by the translators they have to ignore the facts that we have found over 3,000 Greek manuscripts from the second century[2] Then we have the Dead Sea Scrolls, which date from 100 B.C., confirming the accuracy of our Bible.

Honesty demands that the Islamic leaders tell their people the truth - they do not have an infallible revelation from God. They have a collection of contradictions, inaccuracies and preposterous teachings.

Lie No. 2: Muslims and Christians are worshipping the same God

Washington Mayor Marion Barry, who was once jailed for using drugs told the audience at the Million Man March he was thankful to God for his recovery. "The vision for the Million Man March came directly from God himself," Barry told the crowd. "It was God-inspired... Whether we call god Jesus Christ, Yahweh, Jehovah, Allah or just God, he's God."[3]

Mr. Barry holds the position that all gods are the same god, we just call him by different names. That is like saying "America is a government-inspired nation ... Whether we call it democracy, dictatorship, communism or just government, it's government." All gods are no more the same than all governments are the same.

The reason most Americans are not upset over Islam's rapid growth in the United States is they think all religions worship the same God, only using different names. Muslims in America even say Allah and Jehovah are the same god, but that Muhammad is a later prophet of the same god Abraham, Moses and Jesus represented.

Even the Catholic church has fallen for this

deception. The new *Catholic Catcehism* says, "The plan of salvation also includes those who acknowledge the Creator, in the first place amongst whom are the Muslims; these profess to hold the faith of Abraham, and together with us they adore the one, merciful God, mankind's judge on the last day."[4]

It makes some people feel sophisticated to be broad-minded enough to accept all religions as equal. Many have gotten so broad-minded it appears their brains have fallen out.

Only a person who is not familiar with Allah and Jehovah could possibly be deceived into thinking they were the same god. Their differences abound.

Islam says, "Allah loveth not the prodigals" (*Quran* 6:142, Pickthal translation). Jesus, in His story of the prodigal son shows how the God of the Bible loves his prodigal sons (Luke 15:11-24).

The God of the *Quran* is not a father and has had no sons (*Quran* 19:90-92; 112:3). The God of the Bible had a son, Jesus Christ (Matthew 28:19; Luke 3:21-22; John 5:18).

Allah's standard for judgment is that your good deeds must outweigh your bad deeds (*Quran* 7:8-9; 21:47); but the standard of the God of the Bible is nothing less than complete perfection (Matthew5:48; Romans 3:23).

The *Quran* says, "Allah loves not the wrongdoers" (*Quran* 3:139), nor "him who is treacherous, sinful" (*Quran* 4:107). The Bible says the Christian "God demonststrates his own love for us in that: While we were yet sinners, Christ died for us" (Romans 5:8).

The God of the *Quran* declared "no bearer of a burden can bear the burden of another" (*Quran* 17:15; 35:18). But the God of the Bible says Jesus bore the burden of our sins on the cross: "So Christ was once offered to bear the sins of many;

and unto them that look for him shall he appear the second time without sin unto salvation" (Hebrews 9:28).

Allah, the ancient moon god

When Muhammad set out to design a new religion, it was absolutely necessary for him to select a god other that Jehovah, the God of the Jews and Christians. This God was on record as denouncing revolution, slavery, a worldly kingdom and sexual promiscuity. These were the very things Muhammad lived for.

So, with the skill of a crafty Madison Avenue marketeer, he searched for the name of his new god. The Arabian world into which Muhammed was born worshipped 360 pagan gods. The people's favorite was the moon god. Muhammad picked this popular pagan deity and elevated him to the status of "the only true god. This moon god's name was "Allah."

Cesar Farah, in his book *Islam*, establishes Allah as "the paramount deity of pagan Arabia," worshipped from Yemen to the Mediterranean. The moon god was enshrined as the principal god in the pantheon at Mecca. The fact that Allah is the pagan moon god is advertised on the top of every Mosque, minaret, Islamic flag, on the walls of Muslim homes, on their clothing, on caps and on Farrakhan's uniforms. Look and you will see the crescent moon, the symbol of the pagan moon god.

While the deceived masses of Islam deny they are idolaters, the facts prove they are. The *Encyclopedia of Islam* documents the Arabs worshipped a God called "Allah" long before Muhammed was born and Islam was started. (*Encyclopedia of Islam*, eds. Lewis, Menage, Pellat, Schacht, Leiden: E.J. Brill, 1913) Alfred Guilluame, and many other scholars say Arabians worshipped the moon god named Allah![5]

Archeologists diggin in Saudi Arabia have found hundreds of little idols with a crescent moon on their heads. Ancient pagan temples reveal pictures of gods with crescent moons over their heads. The name of this moon god was originally spelled "Al-ilah" which was later shortened to "Allah."

Ancient worshippers of the moon god fasted during the month which began with the appearance of the crescent moon in the sky and closed when that crescent reappeared. They bowed in prayer toward Mecca. The moon worshippers would go to Mecca, run around a pagan stone temple called the Kabah seven times, slit the throat of a sheep and hurl stones at the devil.

Dr. Robert Mory, an outstanding theologian and scholar of Islam, says, "'Wait a second,' you may be saying to yourself, the ancient religious rituals of the Moon God are what the Muslims are still practicing today! The Muslims bow in prayer toward Mecca. They make a pilgrimage to Mecca and run around the Kabah seven times. They are still slitting the throats of sheep and throwing stones at the devil. They even have the fast of Ramadan which begins and ends with the crescent moon. ...what we today call the 'pillars of Islam,' are nothing more than the pagan rituals of the Moon god!"

If one idol, the moon, was not enough, black Muslim Elijah Muhammad declared that the founder of the Nation of Islam, Fard, was god. He said, "The Honorable Elijah Muhammad, I am here to declare, is risen. The Jesus you have been seeking and waiting for His return has been in your midst for 40 years 'but you knew not who he was.' A Holy One was working among us, and it is only now, after he is gone, that we realize who he was.[6]

Farrakhan turns abound and adds another god, by declaring Elijah Muhammad was god, declaring: "But my dear brother and sister, if you bear witness that there is no God but Allah Who Came in the Person of Master Fard Muhammad, and that He is the Best Knower, and that He has raised up The Honorable Elijah Muhammad and fashioned Him into divine wisdom, into the shape of wisdom, his mind being fashioned after the wisdom of God, then you must bear witness that Elijah Muhammad is the best knower amongst us. And if the Messenger permits someone to be in front of you, you should obey Allah and His Messenger and submit to those in authority over you, and Allah will bless you."

So here is the big split in Islam, the mainliners say Farrakhan's crowd is worshipping an idol, while they worship the moon god. Farrakhan says Christians, Jews and mainline Muslims are worshipping a "spook" rather than the true god who lives in a man.

Yet the *Quran* blatantly accuses Christians of worshipping two idols, Jesus and Mary: "And when Allah saith: O Jesus, son of Mary! Didst thou say unto mankind: Take me and my mother for two gods beside Allah?" (*Quran* 5:116). This means Christians "disbelieve" in the true god. "They surely disbelieve who say: Lo! Allah is the third of three.[7] In truth it is Muslims who worship – the Moon god Allah, and in the case of the Nation of Islam, Fard and Elijah Muhammad.

Lie No. 3: Muhammad was
a divinely appointed prophet

Islam is spreading the preposterous lie that Muhammad was a true prophet sent from God. For proof they offer three items: a mole on his back, seizures and a sinless life.

The false sign

Muhammad, himself, offered his followers only one proof he was the prophet of Allah – the sign of a mole on his back. The pagan Arabs thought you could recognize a prophet of god by a seal – a large hairy mole on his back. Muhammad was believed to be a prophet because he had such a growth between his shoulder blades. The *Quran* says: "Muhammad ... is the apostle of Allah, and the Seal of the prophets" (*Quran* 33:40).

The greatest of all the *Hadith* scholars, al-Bukhari, said, "Narrated As-Saib bin Yazid: I stood behind him (i.e. Muhammad) and saw the seal of the Prophethood between his shoulders, and it was like the 'Zir-al-Hijla." (*Hadith*, vol.1, no. 189, vol. 4, no. 741).

The *Dictionary of Islam* explains the "Seal of Prophecy" as: "A protuberance on the Prophet's back of the size and appearance of a pigeon's egg. It is said to have been the divine seal which, according to the predictions of the Scriptures, marked Mahummad as the last of the Prophets ... From the traditions it would seem to have been nothing more than a mole of unusual size."[8]

It is amazing. All the Islamic wars that have been fought, all the converts that have been made flowed from a mole on the back of a man named Muhammad!

Muhammad's seizures

Muhammad also had seizures or spells that at the very first were thought to be epileptic seizures, caused by demons. Later it was decided that god was dealing with him.[9] A good case could be made for reopening the debate.

Jesus Christ offered far different credentials. He said by 'their fruits" you would know a prophet, not by a mole on the back. If a tree has apples growing on it you know it is an apple tree. Men that live holy, godly lives demonstrate their credentials.

Muhammad's "sinless" life

Muhammad's followers have even added to Islam's deception by declaring he was "sinless." This is something so outrageous, even Muhammad never claimed it. And the evidence to the contrary is overwhelming.

Muhammad rose to power on a tide of murder. He called on his followers to kill, rape, plunder and take slaves. Muhammad bragged on the sexual immorality of their prophet. Yet, in trying to present Muhammad as God's prophet, Muslims claim he was sinless.

This presents a contradiction. The *Quran* says Muhammad was a sinner. (*Quran* 42:5; 7:19; 48:1-2; 33:36-38) The *Quran* says Allah told Muhammad to repent. (*Quran* 42:5; 47:19) You cannot repent of sin if you have not been sinning.

"I heard Allah's Apostle saying, 'By Allah! I ask for forgiveness from Allah and turn to him in repentance more than seventy times a day'" (Hadith no. 319, vol. 8, Abu huraira s aid)

During his supposed night journey through seven heavens, Jesus says concerning Muhammad, Muhammad, the Slave of Allah, whose past and future sins were forgiven by Allah" (*Hadith*, vol. 6, no. 3).

The *Hadith* says, "I heard Allah's Apostle saying, "By Allah! I ask for forgiveness from Allah and turn to him in repentance more than seventy times a day" (*Hadith*, vol. 8, no. 319).

Clearly, this modern Muslim claim of Muhammad's sinlessness contradicts the ancient Islamic writings.

Lie No. 4: Jesus Christ
is not our Divine Savior

Islam bitterly attacks the diety of Jesus Christ. The reason is rather obvious. His life and teachings reveal a standard of holiness, kindness and forgivenss that Islam is bitterly opposed to. They demean Christ as an imposter, who was lying when He said *He that hath seen me hath seen the Father* (John 14:9).

But they are very subtle with this lie. Islamic public relation experts conviningly work to pursuade Americans that their religion is very tolerant of other religions, particularly Christianity. *Readers Digest* ran an article by Said Al-Ashmawy, the former Chief Justice of Egypt's Supreme Court, in which he declared, "My Islam is a religion of tolerance and brotherhood."

But the historic record and the *Quran* contradict the idea of tolerance. When Malaysia was under Colonial rule, Muslims said Allah was the same god as the one in the Bible. They simply asked Christians to call their God by the name of "Allah." But as soon as Islamic law was imposed on the country, they made it illegal for Christians to call their god by the name of "Allah."

In Saudi Arabia Christians are likewise forbidden by law to call their God "Allah."

In Jordan, school children get up to four hours a week of obligatory instructions in a 12th grade Islamic religion text which says this about Christian beliefs: "They are clearly idolatrous" and no less "blasphemous" and "false" than those of all other "infidel pagans." It says "Islam cannot reconcile itself to that aberration," and urges that Christians be "forced into submission."

Muslim leaders say woshipping Jesus and the Father is idolatry, insisting there is only one God. Actually the Bible agrees with Islam on the issue of one God: *But to us there is but one God, the Father, of whom are all things* (1 Cor. 8:6). Muslims do not understand that just as H_2O appears in three forms: water, steam and ice, so God appears in three forms: Father, Son and Holy Spirit.

The *Quran* even goes so far as to say the Messiah is the son of Mary (*Quran* 5:17), yet Islam vehemently denies He was the Son of God.

The *Quran* says the crucifixion of Jesus Christ is a lie: "[The Jews] have said, Verily we have slain Christ Jesus the son of Mary, the apostle of Allah; yet they slew him not, neither crucified him, but he was represented by one in his likeness .... They did not really kill him; but Allah took him up into himself." *(Quran* 4:157-58, Sale translation) The reason Farrakhan called the Million Man March "a day of atonement" was they do not believe Jesus Christ has already made atonement for our sins at the cross.

Muslims have circulated a preposterous book denying the deity of Jesus Christ, *The Gospel of Barnabas*. The book, which claims to be the story of Christ, denies Jesus was God and prophesies the coming of Muhammad. The obvious proof it is a fake is the fact that it claims to have been written at the time of Christ but quotes from the *Quran*, which was not written until the seventh century.

The *Quran* declares Jesus a Muslim worshipper of Allah, rather than the son of Jehovah God; "Whereupon the child said, Verily, I am the servant of Allah; he hath given me the book of the gospel, and hath appointed me a prophet. And he hath made me blessed wheresoever I shall be; and hath commanded me to observe prayer, and to give alms, so long as I shall live .... This was Jesus, the son of Mary, the Word of truth, concerning whom they doubt. It is not meet for Allah, that he should have any son; Allah forbid!" (*Quran* 19:30-31, 34-35, Sale translation).

The Bible, in I John 2:22, says anyone who denies the Father and Son is *anti-christ*. Religions that deny Jesus is the Son of God are not neutral toward Jesus. They are opposed to or "anti" Christian.

The *Quran* attacks Christ's teaching that a man is saved by grace and good works are a means of showing appreciation for the gift of grace. But Islam declares a man can be good enough to go to heaven without an atonement for his sins; "On the day of judgment they whose balances shall be heavy with good works, shall be happy; but they whose balances shall be light, are those who shall lose their souls, and shall remain in hell for ever" *(Quran* 23:102-3).

Again, the *Quran* states: "Those that accept the true faith and do good works shall be forgiven and richly rewarded" (*Quran*, 35:7, Dawood translation). Yet the uncertainty always remains as to what measure of works is acceptable to Allah. Those whose works are acceptable will enter a paradise of sensuous, blissful experiences. Those whose works are unacceptable will be damned to serve as fuel for the fires of hell. Judgment and retribution were from the outset a major emphasis in Muhammad's preaching.

Jesus' heaven, where the redeemed fellowship with their loving Savior, is far from the heaven Muslims dream of. The *Quran,* in sharp contrast to the Christian heaven where the glory of God is the attraction, describes a heaven that appeals to the sensual, sexual appetite of carnal men: "In gardens of bliss...(they will be) on thrones, reclining on them, facing each other. Round about them will (serve) youths of perpetual (freshness), with goblets, (shining) beakers & cups (filled) out of clear flowing fountains....and with fruits, any that they may select; and the flesh of fowls, any that they may desire. And (there will be) companions with beautiful, big and lustrous eyes, like unto pearls well-guarded. A reward for the deeds of their past (life)..(this means their past good works)" (*Quran* 55).

Inspite of these vast differences, Farrakhan is trying hard to sell the lie that Islam and Christianity have much in common.

Muslims would do well to read their own *Quran* which says, "See how they invent falsehoods about God. This in itself is a most grievous sin" (*Quran* 4:50, Dawood translation).

The Bible clearly warned us that false teachers would come deceiving masses of people and making much money from it: *There shall be false teachers among you, who privily shall bring in damnable heresies, even denying the Lord that bought them, and bring upon themselves swift destruction. And many shall follow their pernicious ... And through covetousness shall they with feigned words make merchandise of you* (II Peter 2:1-3).

Farrakhan, and the host of Muslim leaders, like so many before them, are using people in their relentless pursuit of property, sex, power and money.

The most tragic result is the millions of poor lost souls littering Islam's battlegrounds. They lived without God and died without God, victims of a ministry of lies.

When Jesus Christ was asked about the signs of his return and of the end of the world, He answered: *Take heed that no man deceive you. For many shall come in my name, saying, I am Christ; and shall deceive many. ... And many false prophets shall rise, and shall deceive many. ... there shall arise false Christs, and false prophets, and shall shew great signs and wonders; insomuch that, if it were possible, they shall deceive the very elect* (Matthew 24:4-5,11-12,24).

Chapter 9
Defusing the time bomb

There is a time bomb ticking in America. The difference between the haves and the have nots is growing increasingly discontent. Farrakhan's Islamic religion is growing, and directing that discontent against white people. The result is that hatred between the blacks and whites is rising to a dangerous level. This situation puts us in a classic condition for riots, terrorism and, in a worse case scenario, even civil war.

Similar Islamic discontent was ignored in Iran and Sudan, and it exploded, destroying both the government and the people's freedoms. America must act now to defuse this bomb before the ticking stops and America explodes. To do this we must adopt a plan to defuse the Farrakhan-Islamic divisiveness and produce a racial harmony that will enable Americans to get along with each other. Islam would not pose a major threat to America if there was racial harmony.

Rodney King's emotional question to his riot torn city of Los Angeles was echoed throughout south L.A.: "Can't we get along?" There is a growing feeling of desperation in our country about finding a plan to inspire the confidence to answer, "Yes! we can get along." So far the nation's search for that plan has turned out to be a long and fruitless one.

Farrakhan, the man millions of blacks are looking to for guidance, certainly has no intention of even trying to unify the races. He is a quitter, a little boy that wants to take his toys and go home. He proposes that blacks give up, separate from whites and have their own country. Unlike Martin Luther King Jr., Farrakhan apparently lacks the faith to believe there can ever be racial harmony. To Louis Farrakhan, King's dream is as an impossible dream.

Farrakhan's Islamic religion offers no hope of racial harmony. Islam's goal is to overthrow all governments and force the laws of the *Quran* upon the entire world. This religion strips people of their freedoms, forces union upon them and results in no tolerance for those who are different. The way Muslims treat dissent, when they gain control, is clearly seen in the Sudan where Islam rules. The black people who refuse to accept Allah as their god are being sold into slavery. In Iraq, the Muslims have slaughtered the Arab Kurds. They have dropped poison gas on them and bombed an entire Kurd village off the face of the earth. Through totalitarian rule, Islam has been able to force some semblance of union upon people, but Islam has never attempted to achieve harmonious unity.

Government, despite its noble efforts, has failed to defuse racial hatred. A solemn front-page warning in the *New Republic*, following the L.A. riots, said: "What we have just witnessed in Los Angeles is a glimpse of a racial and urban crisis in this country that is steadily growing in intensity. Neither Republican neglect nor traditional Democratic liberalism comes close to solving it." Government, at its best, might see to it that all races are treated equal by schools, employers, and the judicial courts. But government cannot change hatred to harmony.

Yugoslavia provides a front page illustration of government's power to suppress racism, but not to solve it. President Tito governed this racially divided country by suppressing their bitter hatred with fear of the gun. From 1945 until Tito died in 1980, the fragile federation of Bosnian Muslims, Serbs, and Croatians was held together by the strong military power. Soon after his death it began to unravel.

On June 25, 1991, Croatia and Slovenia declared their independence from Yugoslavia. Federal troops, made up mostly of Serbs, poured into Slovenia. In 1992 the fighting spread to Bosnia.

Without Tito's iron-handed military control, militants on all sides started training just as the American militia groups are doing here. Suddenly, centuries of deep seated racial hatred exploded into a war that produced the worst atrocities in Europe since World War II. Nothing could stop the fighting between the Serbs, Croatians and Bosnians except a return to the "gun." This time, instead of Tito's guns, it was the guns of NATO. A heavily armed army of ground troops, which included U.S. soldiers, had to be sent into the Balkans to impose a cease fire on the three bitter racial factions.

Thirty-five years of suppression under Tito did not solve the problem. Government can deal with the symptoms of racism, but the roots of racism are rooted deep in the heart of man, beyond the reach of human authority.

Social evolution offers no hope of unity. Elaine Pascoe, in her book *Racial Prejudiced*, quotes Social Darwinists as saying, "Primitive races were held to be incapable of developing the advanced social institutions of whites; to attempt to educate them was fruitless, as their minds were permanently childlike."

America has leaned heavily on education to end racism. Educators hoped they could teach children to respect each other and to get along with each other. I speak to over 50 high school age groups a year and when you listen to them it becomes apparent that racial tensions are increasing in our schools. When I asked a Louisiana group what the biggest problem they faced in their school, a senior spoke up and said "racism." The group agreed with this answer and even the optimism of youth seemed to find no hope for harmony. Education is wonderful for developing the mind, but it only affects the mind, while racism is rooted deep in the passionate, human heart.

The riot torn city of Los Angeles gives us brightly lit proof that other promising plans fail to deliver harmony. Money cannot do it. Minorities in Los Angeles received the most generous welfare payouts. Yet, it turns out, money was not the messiah that could lead Los Angeles out of the wilderness of racial hatred.

Laws cannot do it. Unlike some other parts of the United States, Los Angeles' law had never allowed segregation. Her anti-discrimination laws were as strong as legislators could make them. But government's laws could not bring harmony to the hearts of her citizens. Minority rule cannot do it. When Los Angeles blew up it had a black mayor, Tom Bradley in its highest office.

For many Americans the search for an answer to our racial problems ends with blame. Farrakhan blames the whites for black slavery and suppression. The Ku Klux Klan blames the blacks for being irresponsible parents, and welfare free-loaders. However, the facts are we have people with serious problems and we have to do something about it before it explodes in a bloody civil war. Arguing over who is to blame is useless. Finding a solution is essential.

King's question, "Can't we get along," finds a positive "yes" in the teachings of Jesus Christ. He offered a three-fold plan that has proven it can change the most radical racist. If Americans will launch an all out effort to follow this effective plan America's diverse races can get along. We can work together, in harmony, to build a great united country that will benefit all of the people and be an example to all of the world.

Christ's plan calls for us to do four things. These will meet the challenge of Farrakhan and his Islamic religion: The first is to be changed in our hearts by the supernatural power of God.

1. Be changed by the power of God

As a boy growing up in South Louisiana, racism came easy for me. It was the most natural thing in the world to join in with the other boys for a Saturday night sport we called "nigger-knocking." A half-dozen excited boys would pile into a car with a short log 10 or 12 inches in diameter. We would wait until the blacks made their way down from the theater balcony after the evening movie and started walking the dark country roads home. Then we would make our move. Easing up behind them, we would stick the log out of the back window, speed up the car and hit them in the back of the head. The idea was to knock them out.

One night the victim was an old man who took a real hard lick. The next day we learned he was in the hospital in bad shape. We also learned who the black victim was. To my astonishment we had knocked out the great old fellow who used to take us fishing. He was a friend, someone I really admired and liked. That night, in a frenzy of racial hatred, he was just a black man who needed to be knocked out. This was the first time I felt a twinge of conscience. But he survived and recovered, and my guilt feelings passed.

The second bit of conscience came when I watched the

town marshall pistol whip a drunk, black man. The victim did not fight back, or even resist. But there was no mercy. The lawman just kept pounding his pistol butt against his head until it was a bloody mess. His skin was black, but his blood was red, just like mine. This brutal scene bothered me, but again, I got over it.

These experiences did not change my hateful heart, they only troubled it. The racism just became more embedded with the passing years until I was twenty-years-of age. My wife and I drove to Jackson, Mississippi to attend an evangelistic crusade. The message that night was on, "Ye must be born again." I had never heard this quote from the Bible, even though I had been raised in church. The preacher explained that true Christianity was not merely trying to live by a set of rules, or joining a religious organization. It was a personal relationship with a living Jesus Christ. That night I responded to the evangelist's invitation. A watch repair man counseled me, reading John 1:12, "As many as received Him to them gave He power to become the sons of God." I prayed, asked Christ to come into my heart and experienced a revolutionary change in my life.

A process of growth began that night as God enrolled me in His classroom. First, the Lord showed me I was just a no-good sinner – that I was an *unclean thing,* and that my righteousness was *"as filthy rags"* (Isaiah 64:6). I was in no position to be looking down on anyone, regardless of their conduct, or their color.

God gave me an interesting lesson in Belize, when the Central American country was about 99% black. Walking down the street one day, a group of young blacks sneered at me as I passed and one of them said, "Dirty white trash." I had to laugh and say, "Thank you Lord. Now I understand what it feels like."

When I say that Jesus Christ is the answer to racial hatred I am speaking from experience. The supernatural power of Christ's Holy Spirit can revolutionize the heart of man and bring an end to hatred. Christ emphasized that man must be "converted," or "born again." God had promised this thousands of years ago, *And I will give them one heart, and I will put a new spirit within you; and I will take the stony heart out of their flesh, and will give them an heart of flesh* (Ezekiel 11:19). Instead of working for a political kingdom, as Muhammad taught, Christ said, *the kingdom of God is within you.* This heart changing Gospel of Jesus Christ offers us our hope of averting severe violence in America (Luke 17:21).

My confidence in Jesus' ability to change a racist, soared after meeting Frank Matthews in Birmingham, Alabama. This former black gang leader, testifies, "If anybody has cause in America to be bitter, racist, Frank Matthews did. It was a white officer that took me from my home. My very first jail experience ... I was placed in that county jail. This white man put me in this shower, turned the hot water on and told me to 'tap dance little Nigger.' I've been beat and stomped in them jails by white officers. If anybody had a reason to hate whites, I had that reason. And I had that reason for 15 years. To me I had a chip on my shoulder, I had a reason to hate whites, because they had just done me wrong, messed up my life.

"But when Jesus Christ came into my life, he took away the bitterness, He took away the racism, He took away the hate, He took away the judgment against the white race. And he gave me such a measure of love for the white race that I can't even comprehend it. I can't understand it. Now that is what Jesus can do. What's the panacea? What's the solution for the world's pollution? It is Jesus. If it is racism, Jesus wipes out the racism. The love of Jesus will do it. The love of Jesus is the common denominator that can blend us all and mold us all and make us all one in Him."

A young, black man who lost his job after his place of work was burned down in the L.A. race riots told me, "I do believe there has to be a harmony of the hearts. Actually, there is a lot of greed and tension and stress that is causing people to separate. I really believe there is going to have to be something (to bring) together the ethics and the culture. I think people are going to have to get into the internals and not so much as the external that man can come together as brothers and a people."

This young man put his finger on the real issue, "the internals." Jesus Christ said all evil proceeds from the inside, *out of the heart* (Matthew 15:19). Christ said, *A good man out of the good treasure of his heart bringeth forth that which is good; and an evil man out of the evil treasure of his heart bringeth forth that which is evil* (Luke 6:45). This is why the Bible warns, *Keep thy heart with all diligence; for out of it are the issues of life* (Proverbs 4:23).

Trace the roots of racial hatred and they always lead down inside the heart of man. Proverbs 13:10 says, *Only by pride cometh contention*. The Bible declares all contentions are a result of pride in the heart. When an arrogant husband plays "god" it causes contentions in the home. When an arrogant athlete claims all the glory it causes contentions in the team. When an arrogant gang wants to prove its superiority over another gang, war breaks out. When arrogant citizens feel they are better than others, you are going to have contentions in the nation.

Dr. Durant, an Afro-American professor at L.S.U.,

points out the folly of racial pride; "If the only thing that I can say about myself is that I am black, then I don't have too much to offer myself or society. And if the only thing that a white person can say about themselves is that they are white, then I submit that they do not have too much to offer to society."

Pride in the hearts of men is a problem that has always been around. The ancient Chinese proclaimed themselves "superior" and slurred all other races by calling them "barbarians." A third century Chinese text describes a race of blonde-haired, green-eyed barbarians that the Chinese said descended directly from monkeys.

Adolf Hitler claimed pure-blooded Aryans were the superior race. The contentions that resulted from this one man's arrogance resulted in the bloodiest war in history.

Today, Japan denies citizenship and other privileges to the "inferior" Koreans living in their country and the two countries live under a cloud of contention.

Islam is a religion that inflames this kind of pride, increasing contentions. The *Quran* teaches that men can actually be good enough to go to heaven. The *Quran* says, "On the day of judgment they whose balances shall be heavy with good works, shall be happy; but they whose balances shall be light, are those who shall lose their souls, and shall remain in hell for ever" (*Quran* 23:102-3).

This is quite different from the humbling Christian religion that teaches, *For by grace are ye saved through faith; and that not of yourselves: it is the gift of God: Not of works, lest any man should boast* (Ephesians. 2:8-9). Christianity produces humility and gratitude. It says no one can ever be good enough to go to heaven. It is given as a free gift of God's grace. Our works are done out of gratitude for this goodness to unworthy sinners.

Farrakhan goes to great extremes to encourage pride. He tells his followers blacks are the "superior" race, destined to rule the world, after all the "white devils" are destroyed. Out of this pride comes more racial contentions.

Jesus Christ improves race relations by humbling the proud, contentious heart of man. The Apostle Peter was an arrogant, I-am-better-than-you Jew. He was so filled with prejudices against Gentiles he refused to go and preach the Gospel to them, believing they were too "unclean" for him to associate with. But God changed Peter's heart: "God hath shewed me that I should not call any man common or unclean" (Acts 10:28). When Peter was humbled his eyes were open to see that Gentiles were not just "dirty dogs." They were people God created and Jesus died for.

The great, historic illustration of the power of God to change the heart of man is the conversion of John Newton. This slave trader was carrying a ship load of black slaves to the new world when a storm hit. Newton, in fear of losing his life, turned to Christ. His slave trading ended, his attitudes toward other races was changed and he left us the song *Amazing Grace* as a testimony of how Jesus Christ had changed his life. It is also a testimony to the best way to stop slavery – preach the powerful gospel of Jesus Christ and convert the slave traders!

Donald K. Hyde, an Alabama law enforcement officer during the civil rights march, is proof that the power of God can convert the worst of racists. Hyde grew up in a Christian family, attended church regularly, worked as a deputy sheriff, a city police officer, a state trooper, a federal agent with the U.S. Customs Service and with the Drug Enforcement Administration and through it all remained a bitter racist. "During the time that I was a law enforcement officer in

Alabama, I hated people whose skin was a different color from mine," Hyde said. "I didn't just dislike them – I hated them, and I treated them in ways that showed my hatred. I had done some repulsive things during the 1965 civil rights march."

In time Donald Hyde realized something down inside him was wrong. In 1978 he heard an evangelist tell that Jesus came to change hearts from hatred to love. "It was then that I recognized the hatred inside me," Hyde related. "I asked Jesus Christ to be the Lord of my life – on His terms, not mine. ... I became alive, and the love of God replaced the hate in my life."

Many years later Donald was asked to speak to pastors in the Dexter Avenue King Memorial Baptist Church in Montgomery, Alabama. The black pastors knew him as a dedicated Christian businessman. They had no idea of his past racist life. When he arrived at the church he looked across the podium and saw a mural depicting events of the civil rights movement. When Hyde got up to speak he said, "imagine my surprise when I saw a representation of myself in that mural." Then he confessed how he had mistreated blacks during the 1960s. Bryan said God prompted him to ask the blacks to forgive him. They did. "Since that day five years ago, as God has brought across my path people whom I've offended, I try to set things right. I ask for people's forgiveness. I can't describe the relief, the rest, the freedom from the emotional jail cell that I had put myself into." This is the power of the Gospel of Jesus Christ.

2. Be a witness to the world

It is time for the black and white Christians of America to dedicate themselves to doing what Christ said in His Great

Commission, go, *Into all the world, and preach the gospel to every creature* (Mark 16:15).

Paul gave his life to fulfilling Christ's commission, convinced that this was the answer for diverse and bitter races. He declared, *So, as much as in me is, I am ready to preach the gospel to you that are at Rome also. For I am not ashamed of the gospel of Christ: for it is the power of God unto salvation to every one that believeth; to the Jew first, and also to the Greek* (Romans 1:15-16).

The Bible says the Gospel of Jesus Christ does not come in word only, but in *power* and in the *Holy Ghost and in much assurance* (I Thessalonians 1:5). History has demonstrated this. A true conversion changes the heart, ends hatred, and gives the convert a love for all people: red, and yellow, black, and white.

The Gospel of Christ must be presented to the white churches and the black churches. Church membership is not enough to change men's hearts. People need to be converted by the power of God.

The Gospel of Christ must be presented to Muslims. These people have been deceived into believing in a false religion. The best defense against Islam is a good offense. The booklet, *Christian Witness Among Muslims* says to focus on three truths when witnessing to Muslims: First, The people of Jesus' day rejected Him and plotted to kill Him because he confronted them with their sins: *He is despised and rejected of men; a man of sorrows, and acquainted with grief: and we hid as it were our faces from him; he was despised, and we esteemed him not* (Isaiah 53:3). Muslims agree that those same sins are ruining the world today.

Second, the sinless Jesus gave Himself as a voluntary sacrifice for the sins of all men, as was predicted by the prophets. *He was wounded for our transgressions, he was bruised for our iniquities: the chastisement of our peace was upon him; and with his stripes we are healed. All we like sheep have gone astray; we have turned every one to his own way; and the* LORD *hath laid on him the iniquity of us all* (Isaiah 53:5-6) .

Third, point out that the death and resurrection of Christ provided forgiveness and cleansing to all men: *God commendeth his love toward us, in that, while we were yet sinners, Christ died for us. Much more then, being now justified by his blood, we shall be saved from wrath through him* (Romans 5:8-9). The power of this message will convert the hearts of men and give them love for each other.

We must present the Gospel on college campuses. Lonely college students, away from home, are being recruited at Muslim centers on America's college campuses. Eighty thousand students from Islamic countries are on American campuses building relationships and introducing many to Islam for the first time. A different and strange religion is often appealing to many young informed students. Muslim student unions are popping up on campuses across the country to facilitate Muslim worship and the recruitment of converts.

We must present the gospel to children. Kids are effectively recruited by high profile converts like Mike Tyson and Kareem Jabar to attract youth to Islam. When they change their names they become walking billboards for the Muslim faith. Youth who want to wear the tennis shoes and T-shirts of their sports heroes are also attracted to their religion. We must give them a far greater hero in Jesus Christ.

Meeting the challenge

Islam, though the youngest of the three great

monotheistic religions, has grown to 1.16 billion adherents worldwide – nearly a fourth of all the people on earth today. The Population Reference Bureau reports it is growing eight times faster than the population in developed countries like the United States.

Louis Farrakhan is stressing reproductive expansion. He told the African American Summit in 1989 in New Orleans, "with our increased birthrate, black men and women can breed ourselves into power. They are certainly making progress at this.

Those who are impressed with religious architecture are recruited in the stately Mosques springing up in all of America's major cities. Some of the funds for these expensive edifices come from Arab oil money.

Illegal Muslim aliens are reported to be pouring across our border from Canada, running up the Islamic numbers.

Islam has replaced Christianity as the fastest growing religion in the world, and appears set to replace us as the largest very soon. Islam has replaced Christianity as the fastest growing religion in the United States. The only way to meet the challenge is to put our main thrust in evangelism. We must get out into the highways and hedges Christ and win people to Christ, as Christ ordered us to.

3. Be a good Samaritan
to those in need

My grandmother knew what to do about racism. As soon as I was old enough to drive, it became my duty to take her on her annual Christmas morning trips. As busy as she was cooking for the big family get together, before any food was put on our table, we would have to load up a huge amount of the best food and carry it to some needy black families.

As a boy I thought my grandmother's behavior was just a curiosity which I did not understand. Now, I realize it was a godly Christian woman obeying Jesus' teaching to be a "good Samaritan."

Here is the powerful teaching that has touched hearts and changed people through the ages: *A certain lawyer ... willing to justify himself, said unto Jesus, And who is my neighbour? And Jesus answering said, A certain man went down from Jerusalem to Jericho, and fell among thieves, which stripped him of his raiment, and wounded him, and departed, leaving him half dead. And by chance there came down a certain priest that way: and when he saw him, he passed by on the other side. And likewise a Levite, when he was at the place, came and looked on him, and passed by on the other side. But a certain Samaritan, as he journeyed, came where he was: and when he saw him, he had compassion on him, And went to him, and bound up his wounds, pouring in oil and wine, and set him on his own beast, and brought him to an inn, and took care of him. And on the morrow when he departed, he took out two pence, and gave them to the host, and said unto him, Take care of him; and whatsoever thou spendest more, when I come again, I will repay thee. Which now of these three, thinkest thou, was neighbour unto him that fell among the thieves? And he said, He that shewed mercy on him. Then said Jesus unto him, Go, and do thou likewise* (Luke 10:25-37).

Of course, this teaching is in stark contrast to the me-first philosophy of our me-me generation. Like the priest and the Levite, men callously walk by those in the ditches of life, concerned only with their own welfare. Jesus ordered His followers to shift their attention from themselves to others, particularly the needy. Philippians 2:4 says, *Look not every man on his own things, but every man also on the things of others*. I Corinthians 10:24 says *Let no man seek his own, but every man another's wealth*. The good Samaritan was an example of a man obeying the Biblical command to, *Honour all men* (1 Peter 2:17). Expert sociologist Jack McDevitt stated it this way, "we have to start valuing other people."

There were good Samaritans working in the Los Angeles riots. In the aftermath of the L.A. race riots an airborne television camera captured the ferocious beating of Reginald Denny. This white truck driver just happened to be driving through South L.A. at the wrong time. A mob of angry black men drug him from his truck and beat him, and viciously kicked him in the head. There is little doubt that Denny would have died if three black, "good Samaritans" had not risked their lives, run into the street and rescued the severely beaten truck driver. The worst race riot in American history not only showed us the horrors of hatred, it also showed us the solution – being good Samaritans when we see others in need of our help, regardless of their color.

One day the disciples of Jesus Christ marveled as he broke through the racial fences of the Jews by stopping to help a low class "Samaritan." She was astonished he breached the racial wall by asking her for a drink of water: *How is it that thou, being a Jew, askest drink of me, which am a woman of Samaria? for the Jews have no dealings with the Samaritans* (John 4:9).

Christ tore through the wall of racism to heal the woman's broken heart. As a result many Samaritans came to Jesus as his love unleashed its unfailing force and the barriers of hatred came crashing down.

4. Be a turn-the-other-cheek
Christians to those who wrong you

Ex-gang leader Joseph Jennings, an Afro-American, told a Los Angeles high school assembly, "It was a letter from, someone said the Klu Klux Klan wrote it, you read that letter? 'Yea.' And it said, let me just paraphrase, and it was suppose to be written by the KKK and it went on to say they salute and congratulate all the gang bangers because of the killing of all the young people they are doing. And the letter went on to say in case you can't read this letter go pull a trigger and kill a nigger." Jennings urged the audience to stop making the Klan happy by killing and to start forgiving. This is smart. It is exactly what Jesus commanded His followers to do.

Christ proclaimed this radical approach to harmony; *Whosoever shall smite thee on thy right cheek, turn to him the other also* (Matthew 5:39). He amplified this teaching by saying if a man sued you and took your coat, turn the other cheek and give him your cloak also. And when the Roman soldiers ordered us to carry their heavy shield for a mile, Christ said turn the other cheek and carry it a second mile.

When men turn against you and plot to harm you Christ said turn the other cheek and love them: *Ye have heard that it hath been said, Thou shalt love thy neighbour, and hate thine enemy. But I say unto you, Love your enemies, bless them that curse you, do good to them that hate you, and pray for them which despitefully use you, and persecute you; That ye may be the children of your Father which is in heaven* (Matthew 5:43-45).

Booker T. Washington the first President of Tuskegee Institute in Alabama was walking down the street one day when a wealthy, white, aristocratic woman cried out, "Come here, boy, I need some wood chopped. Without a word, Washington peeled off his jacket, picked up the ax and went to work, not only cutting a pile of wood but carrying it into the house. No sooner than the school president left, one of her servants said, "That was Professor Washington, ma'am." The embarrassed lady rushed to the school and apologized to the gentleman she had ordered to cut her wood. Booker Washington replied, "there's no need for apology, madam. I'm delighted to do favors for my friends." The woman became one of his schools most generous supporters.

Washington could have easily refused to cut the wood, resented the lady's order, denounced her as a racist and started a fight against whites. But this devout Christian was wise enough to follow Jesus' command *Whosoever shall smite thee on thy right cheek, turn to him the other also...Love your enemies, bless them that curse you, do good to them that hate you* (Matthew 5:39,44). Instead of winning an argument, this cheek-turner won a supporter.

It was Booker T. Washington who originated the often quoted line, "I will permit no man to narrow and degrade my soul by making me hate him."

Washington urged blacks to work for a conciliatory relationship with whites. He insisted that black men "cast down your buckets where you are" in vocations such as mechanics, commerce, agriculture and domestic service. He was for a "work your way up from the bottom approach." It had worked for him.

Dr. Durant said, "Many of the black youth today are not looking at the non-violent approach. They are saying, 'Okay then if you smite me on the cheek, then I am going to smite you on the cheek. And I think they are taking a kind of hardened position."

Hating those who sin against you leads to strife. But loving them; pardoning them, covers the matter.

Jesus Christ practiced a pardoning that packed unifying power. He pardoned His own murderers, praying "Father forgive them for they know not what they do." Through Jesus we can have that power. Jesus was a member of the most persecuted race of people in the history of the world. He grew up amidst racial hatred. He understood it. He warred against it.

A Korean bookstore owner said to me, in the aftermath of the Los Angeles race riot of 1992, "I think that Americans have to go back to the Bible. That is the only thing that can solve the racial problems in the United States."

John Holland said, "Science can make a neighborhood of the nations, but only Christ can make the nations into a Brotherhood."

A proven solution to the race problem is put forth in the book: *More Than Equals: Racial Healing for the Sake of the Gospel,* by Spencer Perkins and Chris Rice.[1] Through decades of experience in race relationship they communicate their solution in three words: "admit," "submit," and "commit."

By "admit," they are saying "both white and black Christians must admit that a separation exists, that our relationship is uneasy and that it misrepresents what God intended for his people."

By "submit," they mean "we must hand ourselves over to God, falling on our faces before him for help, recognizing that we can't be healed apart from him."

And by "commit," they mean "deep and lasting reconciliation will be realized only as we commit ourselves to an intentional lifestyle of loving our racially different neighbors as ourselves."

Jesus said, *Blessed are the peacemakers: for they shall be called the children of God* (Matthew 5:9). Those who work to make peace will be "blessed," or happy, knowing they are making a contribution to defusing a bomb threatening to bring devastation to this generation. Someday, up in heaven they will be known as "the children of God."

Index

1. *AP*, February 22, 1996
2. *USA Today*, February 19, 1996, p. 3A
3. *USA Today*, February 27, 1996
4. *AP*, February 11, 1996
5. Washington Times, February 26, 1996, p. A20
6. *AP*, February 10, 1996
7. *AP*, Feb. 26, 1996
8. *PRNewswire*, February 27, 1996
9. Cal Thomas' syndicated column, February 1, 1996

Chapter 2
1. Dr. Anis A. Shorrosh, *Islam Revealed*, p. 185
2. *The Washington Times*, Friday, February 23, 1996, p. A1
Chapter 3
1. *Newsweek*, October 30, 1995, p. 30
2. Henry J. Young, Major Black Religious Leaders Since 1940 (Nashville: Abingdon, 1979, 66-67
3. 7 Speeches of Louis Farrakhan
4. *USA Today*, April 24, 1989, p. 2A
5. Penelope McMillan and Cathleen Decker, "Give us Economic Freedom, Farrakhan Asks." *Los Angeles Times*, October 15, 1985
6. *Newsweek*, October 30, 1995 p.42
7. *Newsweek* October 30, 1995 p.42
8. Elijah Muhammad, *The Fall of America*, quoted in *Vibe*, February 1996, p. 73
9. Michael A. Fletcher, The *Washington Post*, February 24, 1996
10. Charles Rangel, "Denunciation on Demand Ruins Black-Jewish Links. *The Amsterdam News*, October 12, 1985
11. "Black Leader Plans Tour to Counter Farrakhan," *Los Angeles Times*, October 14, 1985
12. Carl Rowan, "Louis Farrakhan: Why Do We Enhance His Hate?," *Los Angeles Times*, September 26, 1985

13.*USA Today*, October 20, 1995, p. 12A
14.Broadcast of March 11, 1984 Again, Farrakhan said in a public broadcast, "Hitler was a genius," Speech of March 9, 1994
15.*Baton Rouge Morning Advocate*, October 26, 1995, p. 10B

Chapter 4
1.*National Affairs*, October 30, 1995
2.*USA Today*, April 24, 1989, p. 2A
3. *7Speches of Louis Farrakhan, p.112*
4. *7 Speeches of Louis Farrakhan*, p. 117
5. *7 Speeches of Louis Farrakhan*, p. 128
6. *7 Speeches of Louis Farrakhan*, p. 128
7. *7 Speeches of Louis Farrakhan Speeches, p. 103*
8. *Speeches of Louis Farrakhan*, p. 113
9.*King Fahd Holy Quran* footnotes, p. 28
10.Speech of Jan. 24, 1994
11.Speech of March 9, 1994
12.Speech of July 26, 1994
13.*Reuters News Service*, November 12, 1995
14.Confronting the Farrakhan problem, *Chicago Tribune*, October 23, 1995
15.*Ibn Hazm*, vol., Part 9, p. 469
16.*Malik ibn Anas*, Vol. 2, p. 155
17.*The Secret Relationship Between Blacks and Jews*, published by The Nation of islam, p.19
18.*Ministry of Lies*, p. 13
19.*Ministry of Lies*, p. 14
20.Professor David B. Davisof Yale University, *Slavery and Human Progress*, 1984, p. 8
21.*Newsweek*, May 4, 1992, p. 32
22.The Economist, June, 1990, p, 42
23.*Newseek*, October 30, 1995, p. 34
24.*Utne Reader*, July/August 1992, p. 81,82

Chapter 5
1.*7 Speeches by Louis Farrakhan*, pp. 68,73
2.George J. Church, *Time* magazine, May 11, 1992
3.Time, may 11, 1992, p. 20
4. *Time*, May 11, 1992, p.26)
5. *Nation*, June 1, 1992
6.*Financial World*, May 26, 1992, p. 76

Chapter 6
1. Ibn Hazm, Al-Muhalla, *The Sweetened*, pp. 458-460
2. Prodigy Services Co., November 16, 1995
3.*Jalalan*, p. 79)
4. *The New York Times Magazine*, March 10, 1991, pp. 26-46
5. quoted in *Behind the Veil*, p.120
6.*Kash-shaf of al-Zamakhshari*, Vol. 1, p. 525
7. *al-Bukhari*, Part VII, pages 145-146
8. *al-Liwa al-Islami* newspaper, July 9, 1987, p. 6
9.*Newsweek*, May 4, 1992, p. 32
10.*Reader's Digest*, January 1996, p. 158
11.Dashti, *23 years*, ppl 120-138

Chapter 7

1. *Seven Speeches*, by Louis Farrakhan, p. 68

2. Ayatollah Murtada Mutahhari, quoted in *Jihad and Shahadat*, Iris, p.105

3. Ayatullah Sayyid Mahmuc Taleqani, quoted in *Jihad and Shahadat*, Iris, p.61

4. Ayatullah Murtada Mutahhari, quoted in *Jihad and Shahadat*, Iris, p.97

5. *In These Times*, Nov. 6. 1991

6. *Seven Speeches*, by Louis Farrakhan, p. 68

7. Ian M. Rolland, *Vital Speeches of the Day*, April 1, 1995, p.377

8. Dr. Muhammad Said al-Buti, *The Jurisprudence of the Biography*, pp. 323, 324

9. Ibn Hisham, *The Biography of the Apostle*, part 4, page 134

10. Isma'il Ibn Kathir, *The Prophetic Biography*, part 3, p. 596

11. October 30, 1995, p.30

12. *The Biography of the Apostle*, part 4, page 134, and also see Al Road Al Anf, part 4, pp. 217, 218.

13. *AP*, November 16, 1995

14. *Time*, February 28, 1994, p. 15

15. Hasan Al-Banna, *Five Tracts of Hasan Al-Banna* (1906-1949), Charles Wendell, Berkeley: University of California Press, 1978

16. The *Baptist Record*, November 5, 1987

17. Washington Times, February 26, 1996, p. A20

18. AP, February 28, 1996

19. *AP* November 16, 1995

20. *Al Wafid Fi Fetouh Al-Sham*

21. Ibn Qayyim al-Jawziyya, *Zad-Al-Maad*, 1081 edition, part 5, p. 90

22. Ibn Hisham, *al-Rawd al-Anaf*, part 4, p. 194

23. bn Hisham, *al-Rawd al-Anaf*, pp. 50, 51

24. *Bukhary*, Vol. 1, p. 13

25. Dr. Buti, *The Jurisprudence of Muhammad's Biography*, p. 287

26. Dr. Muhammad Sa'id Ramadan al-Buti, *Jurisprudence in Muhammad's Biography*, p. 134, 7th edition

27. Abul a'la Maududi, *Jihad in Islam*, Lahore: Islamic Publications, p.198

28. Ruh Allah Khumayni, *Islam and Revolution*, Hamid Algar, tr., Berkeley: Mizan Press, 1981,

29. Time, June 27, 1994, p. 39

30. *Years: A study of the Prophetic Career of Mohammad* London: George Allen & Unwin, 1985, pp. 33-38

31. *Seven Farrakhan Speeches, p. 105*

32. *Seven Speeches*, Minister Louis Farrakhan, *pp. 49, 50*

33. *Al-Kafi*, Vol. III, p. 342; *Wasa'il*, Vol. IX, p. 8

34. Ayatullah Murtada Mutahhari, quoted in *Jihad and Shahadat*, Iris, p.133

35. Ayatullah Murtada Mutahhari, quoted in *Jihad and Shahadat*, Iris, p.128

36. Ayatullah Murtada Mutahhari, quoted in *Jihad and Shahadat*, Iris, p.130

37. *Seven Farrakhan Speeches, p. 105*

Chapter 8

1. Guillaume, *Islam*, pp. 21ff

2. *Geisler & Nix*, page 466

3. *Prodigy News Service*, October 16, 1995

4. *Catholic Catcehism* p. 223, #841

5. Guillaume, *Islam*, p. 7

6. *The Final Call*

7. Pickthall, *The Meaning of the Glorious Koran*, 5:73
8. *Dictionary of Islam*, p. 389
9. McClintock and Strong, *Cyclopedia*, 6:406

Chapter 9
1. *More Than Equals: Racial Healing for the Sake of the Gospel,* by Spencer Perkins and Chris Rice, InterVarsity Press

Printed in the United States
3237